The
NORMAN
TABLE

The NORMAN TABLE

The Traditional Cooking of Normandy

CLAUDE GUERMONT
with
PAUL FRUMKIN

CHARLES SCRIBNER'S SONS · NEW YORK

Dedicated to our parents—
Louise and François Guermont
and Sally and Harold Frumkin

Illustrations by
CHRISTOPHER B. MANSON

Copyright © 1985 Claude Guermont and Paul Frumkin

Library of Congress Cataloging in Publication Data

Guermont, Claude.
The Norman table.

Includes index.
1. Cookery, French—Normandy style. 2. Normandy
(France)—Social life and customs. I. Frumkin, Paul.
II. Title.
TX719.G827   1985   641.5944'2   84-027620
ISBN 0-684-18319-6

1 3 5 7 9 11 13 15 17 19 F/C 20 18 16 14 12 10 8 6 4 2

Printed in the United States of America.

Contents

Introduction

*O*ur days ran long during midsummer in Normandy. The work on my parents' farm often began before the sun had cleared the horizon, ending a dozen hours later, when the light had finally grown too faint to pick out the furrows among the long shadows cast by the hedgerows. One hundred acres under cultivation and a restless collection of cows, sheep, chickens, and other barnyard animals kept the entire family moving from one chore to the next until, by early evening, we would be waning along with the summer light. But even as we bent wearily to collect the remaining few eggs or milk the last cow, convinced that the day would never end, my mother would call us to supper. Swiftly, we would stack the baskets and pails against the barn wall, chase a stubborn goat or two back into their high-fenced pen, and start up the hill toward the house.

If the day's heat still lingered, the family would gather around a narrow wooden table on the edge of our vegetable and herb garden. The color of the sky would deepen, and the evening air cool gently as we sat and talked, with the fresh smells of meadow grass and apple orchards mingling with the savory smells from the kitchen. My mother would carry the meal to the table one course at a time, first setting down a large crock of thick vegetable soup, followed by warm loaves of freshly baked bread and blocks of pale, sweet butter. A platter piled high with slices of lamb roasted pink and flavored with sprigs of thyme and rosemary would come next, accompanied by tender pearl onions and new potatoes still in their skins. Perhaps there might be a cool salad of crisp chicory and cucumber slices, moistened with a vinaigrette redolent of tarragon. For dessert, a choice of warm apple charlotte, rice pudding, or crunchy Norman sugar cookies called sablés. Stirred by this heady offering, my brothers and sisters and I would loudly promote our favorites across the table to one another while my father, only half following the debate, would instead slice off a wedge of Livarot or Camembert cheese to eat quietly with an apple. Cider would be passed around and glasses filled and refilled as the conversation would grow louder and livelier. And for that time, at least, no one grumbled about the long days or the work still to be done.

Farmwork, however, was at the heart of the cooking I was

raised on. From late spring through early fall, my parents' farm demanded long hours of hard work just to keep one step ahead of the moody Norman weather. In return, it provided virtually everything we needed to live independently and well, an exchange particularly in evidence at mealtimes. The flavorful meats and poultry, the fresh fruits and vegetables—all the hearty, filling dishes passed around our table were the result of careful, often laborious tending that gave a special significance to even the simplest foods and also provided us with the sturdy appetites to dispatch them effortlessly. The few odd items we could not raise ourselves we purchased from the crowded stalls of the farmers' market or the tiny shops of the nearby towns. For the most part, however, my family was like the host of other families working small farms throughout Normandy whose larders depended chiefly upon what could be grown or found growing close at hand.

It is this type of modest farm-bred self-reliance that, when interwoven with the province's own remarkable natural abundance, forms much of the basic pattern of Norman cookery. Although shaped in great part by the region's supernal cream, butter, and apples, as well as its renowned fish and shellfish, Norman cuisine is being renewed continuously by a wide array of fine native foodstuffs. On first impression, the Norman countryside suggests an enormous cornucopia that has come uncurled, its bounty spilling out in all directions: fields of wheat and corn roll toward the horizon, suddenly swinging about, now planted with bright strawberries and currants; brown and white cows, grown fat with good living, graze in green meadows cut by fast-running trout streams; earthy-tasting mushrooms push up along the floor of an apple orchard, alive with rabbits and quail; white chickens and fat geese strut stiffly across narrow lanes bordered by wild sorrel and berries; lean brown ducklings peck sharply at loose seeds in lush kitchen gardens.

At the hands of an accomplished Norman cook, whether working in a solitary farmhouse kitchen or two-star restaurant, Norman cuisine can assume many forms. With its great repertory of rich stews, sauces, and pâtés, it can be hearty, as befits the cooking of Viking descendants deeply anchored in a seafaring and agricultural heritage. Or it can be graceful, with elegant dishes of delicate Channel fish and shellfish, flavored only with butter and fresh herbs. Its preparations can take the form of simple roasts and vegetable dishes with their immediately recognizable and reassuring flavors or the more complex form of long-simmering local tripe dishes with their deep, acquired tastes. In any case, Norman cookery possesses, like the Norman people themselves, a unique and imaginative quality that sets it apart from that of the rest of France.

My mother's cooking was pure Norman, learned under the long patient tutelage of my grandmother, who, I imagine, learned her lessons from my great-grandmother—all Norman links in the unbroken chain of handed-down French culinary traditions. Since I loved cooking and had formed some early plans to become a professional chef, I would loiter in the kitchen when work and time allowed, picking up whatever insights I could. During the winter and early spring months, my mother's cooking remained simple, uninspired, balancing salted and smoked meats against dried herbs and home-canned vegetables. Once summer was underway, however, her cooking would burst out of all cold-weather constraints. Each day would find a different dish on the table: veal, pork, duck, or chicken, roasted, grilled, fried, or sautéed, with shallots, apples, mushrooms, leeks, chervil, or crème fraîche. If my brother Daniel had had a successful day foraging in the woods, there might be rabbit braised with chestnuts. Or if we had made a trip to the farmers' market that day, there could be mussels on the half-shell or scallops poached in freshly skimmed cream.

At first I helped in the kitchen with the smaller tasks. I would clean the leeks or shallots or small piles of herbs or perhaps crank the handle of the heavy glass butterchurn filled with thick ivory cream. Later, after I had begun to understand a few of the basics, I cooked, fiddling for hours with my own variations of roast duck or apple tarts. But mostly I just watched my mother. She worked without a cookbook or written recipes; the countless preparations that streamed from her kitchen had all been committed to memory years earlier. One year, for a birthday gift, I bought her a small cookbook, thinking that she could glean some new ideas from it. She thanked me, and I imagined that she was pleased. But then, after flipping quickly through the pages, she placed it on the shelf above the stove. The book wasn't opened again until years later when my sister Nellie, grown up and married, rediscovered it and carried it home with her. So I simply continued to watch my mother as she cooked. And by watching her carefully, I began not only to learn the craft she understood so completely, but to appreciate the cycle that begins in the fields and ends with the richness of the Norman table.

Curiously, this richness is one of the few truly common characteristics of the province. Lying along the top of France, Normandy may be more appropriately considered a cluster of physically distinct areas than a region with any strong prevailing uniformity. To the north is the English Channel and a long broken coastline that encompasses sand dunes, pebbly beaches, soft salt marshes, rocky inlets, and ruggedly beautiful chalk cliffs reminiscent of those at Dover. The Seine empties into the Channel at Le Havre after having meandered for miles in large lazy loops through the easternmost section of the province, its deep, luxuriant valleys in strong relief against the flat, treeless plains stretching out along either side. Called Upper Normandy, this region is dominated by the large-scale farming of wheat, corn, sugar beets, and flax. It is presided over by the city of Rouen, once the capital of the province and today a major port along the Seine. "Paris, Rouen, and Le Havre are a single town," Napoleon once said, "and the Seine is their main street."

Traveling west and south of the Seine, the countryside begins to grow more lush as green hedgerows, freshwater streams, and orderly rows of apple trees break the monotonous sprawl of the land. It was at Giverny, not far from where the Seine enters the province from the Île de France, that the Norman-born painter Claude Monet helped give birth to the impressionist movement by capturing the luminous and subtle qualities of this area in his paintings. The Perche region, famous throughout France for its fine horses, is also an excellent example of this transitional terrain. Directly to the north of the Perche is the Auge Valley, a brilliant sea of green that

is most often referred to as the "garden of Normandy." Dotted
with elegant châteaux and picturesque half-timbered houses
lurching with age, the gently undulating countryside produces
what many claim to be the finest ciders and dairy products in
France. It was here in 1791 that a young farmer's wife named
Marie Harel supposedly perfected the making of Camembert
cheese, forever fixing the valley in every serious gastronome's
atlas.

The province shows a more roughcast face as you continue
west into Lower Normandy. The Suisse Normande is an area
of high peaks, deep valleys, and craggy rock cliffs, while the
windswept Cotentin peninsula, jutting far out into the English
Channel, is buffeted by tides that can retreat farther than the
eye can see. The Bocage, however, where I grew up and where
my family has farmed for generations, resembles neighboring
Brittany more closely than it does the other regions of Nor-

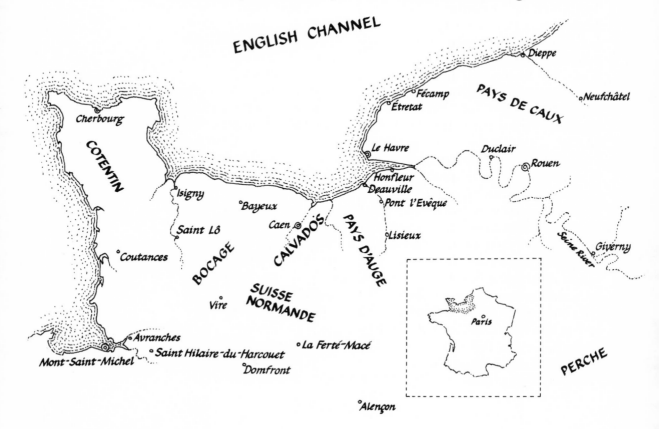

mandy. While similar to the Auge Valley with its apples and dairy-rich farm economy, the Bocage is more densely wooded and rustic, providing a glimpse of an older Normandy before the great forests were cleared for farmland during the Middle Ages.

The strong sense of local pride that pervades France has deep roots in Normandy, and windy discussions are not uncommon when farmers from distant points of the province gather. These debates can range from the merits of each area's politics to more earnest disagreements concerning the quality of local agricultural products. Such meetings, once underway, can produce some interesting arguments. I once heard a farmer from the Auge Valley tell my father a story that must have finally appealed more to his sense of humor than his sense of accuracy.

"One evening before going to bed," the farmer began, "I left a wooden walking stick leaning against the barn wall, one end resting in a newly turned patch of ground. In the morning, when I returned to the barn, I was amazed to find that the stick had sprouted.

"But instead of slicing the sprouts off, I replanted the stick on the edge of the apple orchard—just to see what would happen. "And today," he declared, "I press Auge Valley cider every autumn from the apples I picked from that walking stick."

My father managed the last word. "It's very nice to hear about where your apples come from," he replied coolly. "But how did the cider taste? That's what counts in the Bocage."

During the late summer and early fall, the Norman countryside seems to exhale the breath of apples. They are at the center of Norman tradition, supplanting the wine grape, which makes a poor showing this far north. Numerous varieties abound throughout the area, but the Reinette, russet and streaked with yellow, is certainly queen. Sweet and crisp, particularly when late-harvested in the Auge Valley, it is to apples what the Cabernet Sauvignon is to grapes. Unlike the Cabernet, however, the Reinette's fate is not to be pressed—it is, above all, an eating apple. My parents still grow Reinettes; specifically a popular variation called Reine de Reinettes, as do the majority of the farmers in the Bocage who tend apple orchards. Those apples not immediately eaten or sold are stored away in cool farmhouse cellars to be enjoyed later in the season.

In addition to the Reinettes, our orchards produced small hard Calvilles—used by my mother for baking and pastries—as well as Tête de Brebis, Clos Roger, Machée Rouge, Diard, Douze au Gobet, Saint Lô, and half a dozen more. These my father harvested and crushed every October on my grandfather's wooden cider press. The cider was collected, allowed to ferment slightly, and then quickly bottled and corked. This drink made by the farmers is known throughout the province as *cidre bouché,* or corked cider, and was at one time more popular in the courts of France than wine. Dry and lightly sparkling, corked cider is available year-round in local bakeries or butcher shops, nearly anywhere food can be purchased. Low in alcohol—about 5 percent—it is drunk with virtually every dish imaginable, from the full-flavored duck pâtés and pork sausages to the tiny, delicate Channel clams called coques. In especially fine years my father's cellar of corked cider stands at anywhere from two to three hundred bottles, and he rarely needs an excuse to uncork three or four.

In most years a portion of the apple harvest is sold to the local distillers of Calvados, Normandy's robust brandy. Distilled from fermented apple juice, Calvados is widely appreciated throughout France and recognized as a northern cousin of Cognac and Armagnac. Its enormous popularity in the province has given rise to a tradition called *le trou Normand,* or Norman hole. The hole in question occurs about midway through a large meal at which time all eating ceases so that the diners may quaff a small—or large—glass of Calvados. That done, the meal may then continue. Normans defend this well-worn tradition with the explanation that Calvados aids in the digestion of the meal. Critics glibly suggest an alternative reason: Normans simply love their Calvados.

Professionally distilled Calvados is controlled by the French government in much the same manner as other brandies through the strictly enforced appellation controllée laws. However, many Norman farmers turn a blind eye to the laws and distill their own in homemade copper stills. A. J. Liebling, the American journalist who wrote perceptively about France and Normandy, explains this legal lapse in his book *Between Meals:* "Good Calvados is never sold legally," he wrote. "The tax leaves a taste that the Norman finds intolerable. . . ." These private-label brandies can run the gamut from fierce to sublime, depending upon the distiller's particular recipe or *signature*—in the case of my father's Calvados, hazelnuts are added to deepen the color and flavor as it ages.

But if the apple is close to the heart of the Norman people, it is prized no more highly than the province's milk and cream. Sweet and thick, Norman cream imparts an elegance to the simplest fish and poultry dishes, a quality so widely recognized that the term *à la Normande,* in professional/classical parlance, has come to define a dish flavored primarily with the finest cream available. And yet, while embraced by the classical establishment, Norman cream remains first and foremost the hallmark of the farmhouse kitchen, from whence it has given rise to the fine pale butter of the province and excellent regional cheeses such as Camembert, Livarot, Pont l'Évêque, and Brillat-Savarin. Most small farms in our area of the province maintain at least a few head of the distinctively marked Norman dairy cattle, while the larger farms raise herds, selling their milk through local cooperatives. Even an occasional townsperson will keep a cow tethered in his backyard, milking it twice daily and making homemade butter or farmer cheese or Normandy's genuinely unsour crème fraîche from the rich cream skimmed off the surface. In fact, so rich in butterfat is fresh Norman cream that my mother used to make crème fraîche by simply leaving a crockful in a dark corner of the cellar—or if the cellar was too warm, she would lower the crock down the wellshaft with a rope. In a few days the cream would have thickened naturally and taken on a pleasantly tart flavor. For baking and pastry making, though, Norman cooks prefer to use the milk that has already had the top cream skimmed off. Called fleurette, this sweet cream is considered light by Norman standards; elsewhere, however, fleurette would pass for heavy cream.

While apples and dairy products are staples of Norman

cuisine in general, individual towns and regions are often inclined to take special pride in a food that has been raised
locally. Small tasty ducklings from the area around Rouen and
Duclair are mainstays of many local restaurants, whether
roasted simply with butter and herbs or prepared with a sauce
made from the duckling's blood and finely minced liver. Pears
picked from the orchards surrounding the town of Domfront
are pressed and then distilled into poiré—the British call it
perry—a white wine-pale brandy at one time quite popular in
Normandy but now largely eclipsed by Calvados. Sheep and
lambs pastured in the sandy salt meadows along the Nor-
mandy-Brittany border graze daily on grasses watered by the
twenty-four-hour flood tides of the English Channel and produce meat that is delicate with a lightly salty flavor. It is
reputed to be the finest in France.

To the north, along Normandy's rocky coastline, however,
the emphasis shifts from farming to fishing, and the local fleets
leave for days and weeks at a time from the busy ports of
Dieppe, Fécamp, Cherbourg, Le Havre, and Honfleur. Sweet-
fleshed sole, turbot, cod, mackerel, roussette, chien de mer,
and rouget are hauled from the sea, as well as an abundance
of langoustines, small lobsters the fishermen call demoiselles,
and smaller shrimp called crevettes, which are eaten shell-on
and washed down with chilled corked cider. From autumn
through early spring, fat mussels, oysters, scallops, and tiny
coques are harvested from the beds at Isigny, Villerville, and
Dives. As you travel farther inland, it is not uncommon to find
farmers who rarely eat fish and, even less often, shellfish. In the
coastal towns and cities, however, seafood tops the menu, and
tourists travel from all parts of the country and Europe to dine
on these fresh Norman delicacies.

Early-morning fish markets and auctions are as customary
in these ports as farmers' markets are in the inland towns. Here
auctioneers and fishermen loudly sell their catch to buyers
from the towns and cities farther to the south. Local shopkeep-
ers, restaurateurs, merchants from Paris, and even the occasional tourist can be found milling about the docks as the sun
rises on market days. The sellers are shrewd and move quickly,
for a moment's hesitation and a buyer is lost to the next stall

down the street. At the close of the market, the auctioneers gather at nearby cafés to discuss the day's business over corked cider or white wine, while the fishermen return to their boats and prepare to go out one more time.

Sailing and the sea are as intrinsically bound up in the fabric of Norman tradition as farming, but they appear to have played a more instrumental role in shaping the area's history. While the wide fertile countryside has always promoted the more placid aspects of Norman life, the sea provided adventure and, more often than not, change. During the Bronze Age the province's first settlements sprang up in and along the winding Seine Valley as the river became a crucial link in the ancient Tin Road to England. The ability to control the movement of tin—which when alloyed with copper was used to create bronze weaponry—was necessary to the survival of early civilizations, and their boats plied the English Channel, traveling inland on the larger rivers. The Celts were the first to settle as a group, hunting and fishing in the deep forests and freshwater rivers and streams, raising pigs, sheep, and cattle, and growing wheat and barley. Their cooking methods were simple. Whole animals and large cuts of meat were roasted on spits over smoking wood fires; smaller pieces were boiled in pots full of water. In addition, they supplemented their diets with milk, butter, honey, nuts, and fruit. It was the Celts, some sources say, who began the cultivation of "avals," or apples, in the region.

Under Julius Caesar the legions of Rome conquered and inhabited the province, bringing with them a long civilizing peace. During the following three centuries durable highway systems and strong fortresses were constructed, and the settlement of future Norman cities such as Rouen and Coutances was begun. The Romans also introduced a richer, more elaborate cuisine to the area, and the Celts soon learned about exotic sauces and Eastern spices, cheese and sausage making, and salting meats for preservation. At the same time they tasted many new foods from the warmer latitudes which the Romans attempted to transplant in the cooler Norman climate. Olives and figs failed quickly. The cultivation of grapes met with mixed success. The vines took, but the wines pressed from them could not stand up to the southern vintages supplied from Italy and southern France—good enough for the foot soldiers, perhaps, but for the Roman patricians, not likely.

Following the slow disintegration of the Roman Empire, the Merovingian and Carolingian Franks came to dominate the area. Warlike northern tribes that had been civilized and converted to Christianity, the Franks continued the process begun by the Romans, zealously building a great monastic center in Rouen in addition to smaller monasteries in the other

large towns of the province. The local inhabitants helped to support these splendid centers of learning with their labor and gifts of crops and livestock. When necessary, however, the monasteries could be quite self-sufficient. Monks tended their own kitchen gardens inside the high stone walls, raising leeks, carrots, turnips, radishes, onions, and watercress, plus an extensive variety of herbs for flavoring and medicinal purposes. Hens were raised, but more likely for their meat rather than their eggs. There were small wooden pens for sheep and other domestic animals, including rabbits, which these early monks were the first to domesticate for food. And to ensure a supply of fresh fish, many monasteries were equipped with vivaria, ponds in which freshwater fish such as trout and perch were kept alive.

During this period of religious building, a bishop of Avranches named Aubert claimed to have been visited three times by the Archangel Michael, who commanded him to build an oratory on a great rock in the bay southwest of the town. The first two visits by the angel he ignored, Aubert later told believers. On the third visit, however, the Archangel drove home his point by inserting a finger into Aubert's skull, thereby convincing him of his seriousness of purpose. In the following centuries Aubert's vision would gradually take shape as one of the great architectural and spiritual treasures of Normandy and the world: the Benedictine Abbey of Mont-Saint-Michel.

The civilizing efforts of the Franks were halted, however, in the opening years of the ninth century as fierce Vikings in their black-sailed dragon ships launched the first of many invasions against the province. Attracted by the riches of the monasteries and the countryside, these Scandinavian pirates flooded up the Seine Valley and across the province. Yet, while many of the Norsemen entered the province as pirates seeking treasure and plunder, they were principally farmers, and as such, fell under the spell of the area's natural beauty and dark fertile soil. Soon they were sending for their families, and the Viking settlements grew rapidly.

The eating habits of the Vikings were similar to those of the early Celts, and the countryside was easily able to sustain them. Their daily diets included pork, lamb, and veal, preferably boiled in full-flavored broths containing vegetables such as onions and cabbage. Fish and shellfish were also staples, as were poultry and wild game, which the Vikings hunted in the dense forests of the province. They drank strong beer and sweet fermented mead when they gathered for feasts but kept dairy cows to supply fresh milk and cream at other times. From the cream they made pale soft cheeses and churned sweet butter, spreading it on wholemeal breads made from barley, oat, and rye grains.

To the Vikings, Normandy must have appeared as a paradise after the long, sullen northern winters they had grown accustomed to in their native lands, and it is no surprise that they settled in for a long stay. In 911, a shrewd Frankish king named Charles the Simple perceived the invaders' intentions and persuaded their leader, Rollo, to end hostilities and accept the land his people already occupied. This agreement came to be known as the Treaty of Saint-Clair-sur-Epte, and Rollo became the first Duke of Normandy.

Under Norman rule the province flourished as never before. Rollo and his blue-eyed, fair-haired descendants proceeded to create a brilliant and powerful government that would eventually lead Normandy out of the Dark Ages. As converts to Christianity, the Norman lords restored the monasteries and towns ruined by a century of warfare. They invited the monks who had fled, particularly the Benedictines, to return. Within decades, Rouen, Caen, Bayeux, and Fécamp were once again thriving cultural centers. Military conquests in Britain by William the Bastard (Conqueror to his friends) and in the Mediterranean by the Norman-led Crusaders flooded the province with even greater wealth and power, and for two centuries few medieval states could match the grandeur of Normandy.

During the Crusades extensive trade routes were opened up to the east and south, introducing hitherto unknown herbs, spices, and foodstuffs into the province and propelling Norman cuisine into a period of excessive richness. *Le Viander de Taillevent,* compiled in 1375 by a Norman-born master chef named Guillaume Tirel and thought to be the first cookbook of modern Europe, gives a clear account of the ingredients and techniques of the age. Powerful spices such as nutmeg, cinnamon, mace, ginger, cardamom, and cloves were added unsparingly to dishes. Golden saffron seemed to flavor every recipe from soups to desserts—provided that the family was wealthy enough to afford it. Exotic-sounding purées of poultry and fish were common to the extravagantly laden tables of Norman royalty, as were thick stews, simmered and stirred for days in caldrons suspended in capacious kitchen hearths. There were also flavorful pies prepared by wrapping dough around chopped or puréed meats, combined with vegetables and spices, and then baked in brick ovens.

This immoderate use of spices and the need to obscure natural flavors would gradually give way in Normandy to a simpler approach to cooking, one that would place more emphasis on fresh locally raised ingredients and less on exotic imports. Herbs such as thyme, chervil, parsley, and chives, grown in small kitchen gardens, would replace dried spices from Africa and the Far East. Norman butter would all but eliminate the need for more expensive cooking oils from the south, and the light local ciders, vinegars, and cream would help to create a repertory of rich, yet uncomplicated, sauces.

The farmers' market, however, is one custom that survived the Middle Ages. At one time just a small area cordoned off in the center of a city for merchants and farmers to barter, farmers' markets have continued to grow in size and importance over the years. Today, these bustling colorful marketplaces are held in cities and towns across the province and are chiefly responsible for having popularized many of Normandy's more closely kept delicacies beyond its borders.

On market day in Saint Hilaire-du-Harcouet, farmers, merchants, and casual shoppers flock from miles away to buy, sell, or merely sample the foods they cannot grow or purchase closer to home. My entire family would drive the three or four miles from our farm, help set up my mother's small egg stand, and then break away to wander the crowded streets and gape at the other stalls. Within one block we could ogle a table piled with locally baked breads, brioches, and buttery croissants or gaze hungrily at a stall hung with bunches of tangy pork sausages from the town of Vire. Behind the stall owned by the black-cloaked accordion player who sold sheet music, we might find a small stand filled with sweet apple tarts made by a group of farmers' wives from the Auge Valley. Everywhere we looked on market day, we would find the bounty of Normandy: piles of oysters and clams plucked from the beds outside of Isigny, towers of cheeses from the towns of Pont l'Évêque and Neufchâtel, terrines and pâtés, cider and cream. We would stay hungry for days afterward.

Besides my mother's kitchen, the farmers' market was my next most serious introduction into the cooking of the province. It allowed a glimpse of the Norman cuisine that existed beyond our table and finally helped whet my appetite to learn more. At the age of fourteen I apprenticed myself to the chef of a hotel in nearby Avranches. Although the hotel was small, it catered predominantly to tourists who had come to the area to visit Mont-Saint-Michel across the bay while enjoying a bit of local flavor in the dining room. The hotel's chef, Rosalie Fontaine, was Norman-trained, Norman-proud, and more than glad to give her guests the Norman cooking they were seeking, while good-naturedly exhorting us, her young apprentices, never to strive for anything less than Norman excellence. During my three years at the hotel, she marched us through the preparation and lore of Norman provincial cooking, from the simple dishes of the farmers and fishermen to the more sophisticated recipes of the region's professional kitchens. Although the methodology she stressed was pure Escoffier, her lessons were always marked by strong Norman sensibilities and fine local foodstuffs.

I mention Rosalie here because, after my mother, she is probably the most significant contributor to this book. To be sure, a few recipes were learned in Paris or Provence or even Hyde Park, New York, from other Norman-trained chefs who were glad to swap stories and tastes of home. But no less than two or three dishes from each section, and at least half of those in the fish and shellfish chapter, are based on recipes learned in Rosalie's kitchen.

As for the recipes, I can only hope that they speak for themselves. Good food should. I have *fiddled* with them as little as possible, although changes were inevitable. In certain recipes where an ingredient was known to be unavailable, I have substituted what I felt to be its closest equivalent. In others I have attempted to provide the reader with a choice between a richer, traditional ingredient and a lighter, more contemporary one. In all cases, I have tried to reproduce the original recipe so that it retains as much of its native integrity as possible.

In the end, what is perhaps most important is that these recipes are not be looked upon as museum pieces, frozen in a particular time or place. They have been and continue to be part of a vital living culture and, as such, should not be considered above change. If one ingredient is not available, then experiment with another; if there is a technique that you prefer over one that I have suggested, use it. A recipe should not come with a lock and key. In fact, the very premise of the Norman cookery I was raised on is to prepare the best food possible using those products that are close at hand. To paraphrase my father's answer to the Auge Valley farmer with the amazing walking stick: It's very nice to hear about where the recipe comes from. But how does it taste? That's what counts in Normandy.

Basic Stocks and Sauces

N orman cuisine calls for a variety of ingredients that, only a few years ago, were not widely available in this country. Today, however, such vegetables as fresh leeks, shallots, and artichokes can be found in most large grocery stores, along with sorrel, chives, and various types of fresh and dried mushrooms. Fresh fish and shellfish are sold everywhere, and in some areas it is possible to get fresh game such as rabbit, quail, and partridge. It is more than likely, however, that a few of the ingredients listed here will not be readily accessible in all parts of the country; anticipating this, I have suggested substitutions that match the flavor and texture of the original ingredient as closely as possible. As a general rule, you will quickly find that Norman cooking is not exotic, and no shopping trip should take you too far afield.

NORMAN ESSENTIALS

Before proceeding to the recipes, it is worth taking a close look at some of the more fundamental elements of Norman cooking. Cream and butter, for instance, are used so lavishly in the recipes of the province, that many assume they have always been a cornerstone of the cuisine. Actually, it has only been the past few decades that butter has really been able to stake an uncontested claim to that position. Before that the chief cooking medium was a preparation called graisse normande.

This rich mixture of fats and vegetable essences is one of the great characteristic flavors of the province. In Normandy it was once held in the same esteem as goose fat is today in southwestern France. Although it is used rarely now, graisse normande was at one time considered the signature of the finer cooks of the region, with the proportions and types of fat varying from town to town and farm to farm. Many dishes would have tasted incomplete without it, and in the Manche region of the province, a soup was even created called Soupe à la Graisse.

In the recipes for this book, I have included graisse normande when appropriate; I have also noted when you may replace it with butter. Even for those people who shy away from using such a rich fat mixture, I would suggest trying this Norman specialty the next time you find yourself craving a particularly hearty dish. I think you will find the experience worthwhile.

GRAISSE NORMANDE

8 ounces very firm beef fat, from the kidney area, if possible
4 ounces pork fat
½ cup coarsely chopped onions
1 medium carrot, washed, peeled, and cut into ¼-inch slices, approximately
1 medium turnip, washed, peeled, and cut into ¼-inch slices, approximately

1 medium parsnip, washed, peeled, and cut into ¼-inch slices, approximately
1 leek (green part only), cut into ½-inch lengths
1 small bouquet garni (parsley stems, sprigs of fresh thyme, and 1 bay leaf in a cheesecloth bag)
Salt and pepper

YIELD: 1 TO 2 CUPS

1. Chop the beef and pork fat into small pieces and place them in a heavy pot. Add 1 cup water.
2. Place the pot over low heat, half off the burner or coil, for 2 hours and stir occasionally. The fat will melt and begin to clarify.
3. After 2 hours, add the vegetables and the bouquet garni. Stir, then simmer for approximately 2 hours more, or until the fat is clear and the vegetables have released all their flavor.
4. Remove the pot from the fire and let it rest for about 30 minutes. This will allow the particles to settle to the bottom of the pot. Strain the fat mixture through a fine sieve or cheesecloth once or twice if necessary to remove all the particles.
5. Season the stock with approximately 1½ teaspoons salt and ⅛ teaspoon pepper. Place it in a tightly closed jar in the refrigerator. The mixture will keep for up to 4 months.

For the modern Norman cuisine, however, butter is still the foundation of most recipes. Fresh Norman butter is exceptionally rich, imparting an unmistakable flavor to any dish it graces. Perhaps the finest butter of the region comes from the Auge Valley around the town of Isigny. Butter from this area is available in a few specialty stores and even through certain mail-order catalogs. But take note: Norman butter costs between two and three times more than domestic butter. Still, it may be worth the expense if you want to recreate the true flavors of the province.

Many domestic butters are very fine, but I would recommend using unsalted or sweet butter rather than lightly salted. Once again, the cost is higher, but the flavor is closer to its Norman counterpart.

Another recommendation is that you make your own butter. The process is quite simple if you have a good electric mixer, and the addition of fresh butter to any recipe will heighten the flavor remarkably.

FRESH BUTTER

1 quart heavy cream
Salt

1. Pour the heavy cream into 4-quart mixing bowl of a standing electric mixer. At medium speed whip the heavy cream for 20 to 25 minutes. Note: A hand-held mixer will also work, but be prepared to stand in one place for a while. It can be as tiresome as using a butterchurn—I know, I've used both.
2. After the cream has thickened into butter, drain the liquid that has separated out. This is pure buttermilk and can be used in any number of recipes or enjoyed as is. At this point, taste the butter and decide whether you want to add salt. If you do, season to taste.

YIELD   One quart heavy cream yields approximately 1 pound fresh butter and 1 pint buttermilk.

Another basic ingredient in Norman cooking is beurre manié, an uncooked butter-and-flour mixture used to bring sauces to the proper consistency and texture. At times, the flour in a beurre manié is browned first in an oven so that when it is added to a dark sauce, the color will not lighten. This process is classically based, however, and not really necessary to provincial cooking. Although beurre manié should be stored in the refrigerator, bring it to room temperature before using: it will dissolve more readily in the sauce.

BEURRE MANIÉ

2 tablespoons butter, at
    room temperature
3 tablespoons flour

1. Blend the butter and the flour together in a bowl by hand until smooth. Refrigerate.

This mixture will make enough to thicken approximately 1 pint   YIELD liquid to the consistency of heavy cream. For more, simply double the ingredients.

CRÈME FRAÎCHE

Normandy is the birthplace of crème fraîche, and it is used lavishly in the province as an ingredient in sauces, on vegetables, or even on fresh fruit. Today, crème fraîche is available in any small store in the province, but when I was growing up, every family still made its own.

    My mother's recipe for crème fraîche could not have been simpler: she would begin with cream skimmed from fresh cow's milk, pour it into a crock, and cover that loosely with a towel or cloth. Then, since our cellar remained cool for most of the year, she would set the crock in a dark corner and leave it for three to four days. During this time the cream would thicken naturally, and the flavor would turn slightly acidic. However, our cream was unpasteurized and noticeably higher in butterfat content than the heavy cream sold in the United States—my mother's method won't work with pasteurized cream. The recipe that I have included here calls for two parts sour cream to three parts heavy cream; whether you are working with cups, pints, quarts, or ounces, this ratio never varies. I've experimented with a recipe that uses buttermilk, but have found that adding sour cream will result in a flavor closer to true crème fraîche.

YIELD: 5 CUPS   *2 cups sour cream*
3 cups heavy cream

1. In a bowl whip the sour cream well by hand for approximately 30 seconds.
2. Heat the heavy cream in a saucepan to about 85° F (lukewarm to the touch), stirring constantly.
3. Add the sour cream and mix well.
4. Cover the mixture with a cloth or towel and leave at room temperature (70° to 75°F) for 12 to 15 hours. If you have a gas oven with a pilot light, you can place it in there. Refrigerate when the mixture thickens. Crème fraîche can be kept refrigerated up to 2 weeks.

PUFF PASTRY DOUGH

If puff pastry dough is not Norman by birth, it must certainly be Norman in spirit. Nearly equal amounts of flour and butter folded and rolled six separate times give it an incomparably rich flavor and lightness. I learned this recipe during my apprenticeship, and we used it as an accompaniment or garnish for many of the local seafood dishes. Since I have included a number of those dishes in this book, I also felt compelled to add this recipe. I still feel that well-made puff pastry is the perfect complement to certain dishes. If you are pressed for time, however, many grocery stores now carry individual puff pastry shells in the frozen food section.

8 tablespoons (1 stick)   *1 tablespoon salt*   YIELD: 2½ CUPS
    butter, melted   *3 sticks butter*
3½ cups flour, sifted

1. Mix the melted butter with 1 cup cold water.
2. In a mixing bowl combine the flour, salt, and water-butter mixture just enough to bind the ingredients together in a dough. Transfer the dough to another bowl, cover with plastic wrap, and refrigerate for 45 minutes.
3. Knead the remaining butter by hand until it is soft and pliable.
4. Remove the dough from the refrigerator and place on a floured board or table. Flour the dough slightly and roll it out into a 10-inch square. Spread the kneaded butter over the dough to form a 7- by 7-inch diamond in the center of the square. Fold all 4 corners of the dough into the center so that the butter is sealed in an envelope of dough. Refrigerate the dough for 30 minutes in plastic wrap.
5. Remove the dough from the refrigerator and again place it on a floured board or table, seal side down. Flour slightly. Roll the dough gently into a rectangle that is 8 inches wide by 20 inches high. Brush off any excess flour and fold the top ⅓ toward the center. Then fold the bottom ⅓ over the top. Turn the dough ¼ turn clockwise so the fold is to the right. Roll out again to the 8- by 20-inch rectangle and repeat the folding procedure. Refrigerate for 30 minutes.
6. Repeat Step 5 twice more, making sure to refrigerate the dough for 30 minutes each time.
7. The dough is now ready to use. Extra dough may be kept frozen if wrapped tightly in plastic wrap.

STOCKS

Slowly simmered full-bodied stocks are considered the foundations of classic French cuisine, and in the finer restaurants and hotels their preparation regularly demands the expenditure of time and skilled workmanship. Stock preparation in country cooking differs somewhat, however, in that stocks are rarely made in advance or in any great quantities, and most are prepared in conjunction with other recipes. My mother makes a brown stock only when she is making a roast, adding a few veal bones and vegetables to the meat and then adding water to the pan after the roast has been removed. Her chicken stock is the rich cooking broth saved from a poulet au pot, a fowl or chicken poached with fresh vegetables and herbs.

Since convenience often dictates recipe preparation, it may be easier to have a few quarts of stock on hand rather than waiting to make it until you roast or poach a chicken. The following stocks may be refrigerated for up to one week or frozen for approximately three months.

If you decide to use canned beef or chicken broth, please note that these stocks are high in salt, and any reduction of the liquid will make the dish even saltier. There is really no way to compensate for this other than simply adding less salt at the end.

BROWN STOCK

I have included my mother's recipe for brown stock in addition to a more classically influenced method. Her stock will work with any type of roast—veal, beef, chicken, turkey, and even pork—but the meat should weigh at least 4 to 5 pounds.

VARIATION I
(with a roast)

3 pounds veal or beef bones (meaty, if possible), sawed into 2-inch pieces
3 large carrots, washed and coarsely chopped
3 ribs celery, washed and coarsely chopped

2 large onions, quartered with skin on
Bouquet garni (2 bay leaves, 1 sprig fresh thyme, and 1 tablespoon chopped fresh parsley in a cheesecloth bag)

YIELD: 2 TO 3 QUARTS

1. Place the meat you intend to roast in a large pan and spread the bones and vegetables evenly around it. Roast the meat as your recipe indicates.
2. Once the meat has cooked, remove it from the pan. Transfer the bones and vegetables to an 8- to 10-quart pot and add the bouquet garni.
3. Remove as much fat as possible from the roasting pan, then place it over low heat. Pour about 1 pint water into the cooking juices and scrape up the browned bits from the bottom of the pan. Add to the pot.
4. Add 4 to 5 quarts water to the pot and bring the stock to a boil. Reduce the heat to very low and simmer for three hours, skimming often.
5. Strain the stock by pouring it through a colander into a clean pot or bowl. Cool.
6. Once the stock has cooled, remove the solidified fat and refrigerate.

VARIATION II
(without a roast)

YIELD: 2 TO 3
QUARTS

2 pounds beef or veal
    bones (meaty, if
    possible), sawed into
    2-inch pieces
1 beef shank,
    approximately 2
    pounds
3 large carrots, washed and
    coarsely chopped
3 ribs celery, washed and
    coarsely chopped

2 large onions, quartered
    with skin on
Bouquet garni (2 bay
    leaves, 1 sprig fresh
    thyme, and 1
    tablespoon chopped
    fresh parsley in a
    cheesecloth bag)

1. Place the bones in a roasting pan in a preheated 425° F oven. Roast for 10 minutes, or until the bones render some fat and begin to brown.
2. Stir the vegetables and the bones together, and continue to roast for another 15 minutes.
3. Transfer the bones and the vegetables to an 8- to 10-quart pot. Add the bouquet garni.
4. Follow Steps 3 through 6 from Variation I (above), but simmer the stock for a total of 4 hours.

NOTE   *Rather than discard the beef shank, you may want to use it for the Pommes de Terres Farcies (page 223) or the Chou-Fleur au Gratin (page 216).*

CHICKEN STOCK

The addition of turnips and parsnips gives this versatile stock a decidedly Norman flavor.

4 to 5 pounds chicken wings, backs, necks, gizzards, and trimmings
1 large onion, quartered with skin on
1 large carrot, washed and coarsely chopped
1 rib celery, washed and coarsely chopped
½ cup chopped leeks (green part only)

¼ cup turnip, washed and coarsely chopped
¼ cup parsnip, washed and coarsely chopped
Bouquet garni (1 bay leaf, 1 sprig fresh thyme, 2 cloves, and 1¼ teaspoons peppercorns in a cheesecloth bag)

YIELD: 2 TO 3 QUARTS

1. Wash all the chicken parts in very cold water.
2. Place all the ingredients in an 8- to 10-quart pot. Add 4 to 5 quarts water and bring to a boil.
3. Skim the scum from the surface. Reduce the heat and simmer gently for approximately 3 hours. Continue to skim occasionally.
4. Remove the stock from the heat and strain through a colander. Allow the stock to cool and remove the solidified fat from the top. Refrigerate.

FISH STOCK

For this stock use the frames, tails, and heads from any or all of the following fish: halibut, brill, turbot, bass, tilefish, red snapper, sole, flounder, dab, trout, pike, monkfish, or perch. Soak all fish bones in cold water for 1 hour before using to remove blood and impurities.

YIELD: 1 TO 2
QUARTS

4 tablespoons butter
1 to 2 pounds fish heads
     and frames, cut into
     3-inch pieces
½ cup chopped celery
½ cup chopped onion
½ cup chopped leeks
     (green part only)

¼ cup chopped mushroom
     stems (optional)
1 bay leaf
5 peppercorns, crushed
5 to 6 stems parsley

1. Melt the butter in a 4- to 5-quart pot. Add the fish, cover the pot, and cook over low heat for 5 minutes, or until the flesh of the fish turns white.
2. Add the remaining ingredients, cover, and cook for 5 to 10 minutes.
3. Add 2 quarts cold water. Bring to a boil, reduce the heat, and simmer gently for 30 minutes. Skim occasionally.
4. Strain the stock and refrigerate.

NOTE

One-half cup dry white wine or hard cider may be added to this recipe a few minutes before the water is added. I prefer to make this stock more neutral, adding the wine or the cider to the finished dish later. You may want to experiment with both methods, though.

SAUCES

Even without a locally produced wine, Normandy can still lay claim to two sauces spectacular enough to be included in the exclusive pantheon of classical French recipes: sauce rouennaise, a sumptuous sauce traditionally served with rare breast of Rouen duckling (see Caneton Rouennais à l'Ancienne (page 143), and sauce normande, the velvety cream sauce which, when made with true Norman cream, is incomparable on fish, meat, poultry, vegetables, fruit, or virtually anything you might name.

SAUCE AU VIN ROUENNAISE
A Rich Sauce of Wine, Calvados, and Minced Liver

This variation on the traditional sauce rouennaise omits the duckling blood and the cider and adds red wine instead, rendering the recipe a little more adaptable to other dishes. The wines most often used in Norman cooking are from the neighboring Loire Valley, and a red wine from Chinon or Bourgueil would be excellent in this sauce—although any dry red wine would taste fine. Serve this sauce on sautéed tournedos or any rare breast of game bird.

1 cup dry red wine
¼ cup finely chopped
shallots
1 bay leaf
⅛ teaspoon nutmeg
2 cups Brown Stock (page 27)
1 tablespoon Calvados

4 tablespoons Beurre Manié (page 23)
1 duck, partridge, or pheasant liver, very finely chopped
2 tablespoons butter
Salt and pepper

YIELD: 2 CUPS

1. Combine the red wine, shallots, bay leaf, and nutmeg in a small pot and reduce over high heat until almost dry.

2. Add the brown stock and simmer over medium heat for 10 minutes. Add the Calvados.

3. Quickly whisk the beurre manié into the mixture, making sure to work out any lumps. Simmer for a few minutes more and allow to thicken.

4. Remove the pot from the heat and, vigorously whisk the chopped liver into the mixture. Whisk in the butter.

5. Season with salt and pepper to taste before serving.

SAUCE AU CIDRE ROUENNAISE
A Piquant Variation with Cider and Spices

Once the puréed liver has been added, the sauce must not boil or it will curdle. This is an excellent sauce for red meat or game birds.

YIELD: 2 CUPS

1 cup dry cider
¼ cup chopped shallots
5 peppercorns, crushed
⅛ teaspoon ground cloves
⅛ teaspoon ground allspice
1 teaspoon cider vinegar

2 cups Brown Stock (page 27)
2 duck, partridge, or pheasant livers
2 tablespoons butter
Salt

1. Combine the dry cider, shallots, crushed peppercorns, ground cloves, ground allspice, and cider vinegar in a pot and reduce over high heat until almost dry.

2. Add the brown stock and reduce slowly to 1 cup.

3. Meanwhile, wash the livers and then purée them in a blender or a food processor. Do not cook.

4. When the sauce has reduced, remove the saucepan from the heat and immediately whisk in the puréed liver and the butter. Season with salt to taste.

SAUCE NORMANDE POUR VIANDE
Cream Sauce for Meats

A tangier cream sauce for veal, chicken, and pork dishes. Again, the wine used in this sauce would probably come from the Loire Valley and would most likely be a Muscadet or Vouvray.

3 tablespoons butter
3 tablespoons flour
1 cup Brown Stock (page 27)
2 teaspoons chopped shallots
¾ cup mushrooms, cleaned and sliced

½ cup dry cider or white wine
1 cup heavy cream or Crème Fraîche (page 23)
Salt and white pepper

YIELD: 2½ TO 3 CUPS

1. Melt 2 tablespoons of the butter in a medium saucepan. Stir in the flour and cook over medium heat for 5 to 6 minutes, or until light brown.
2. Stir in the brown stock until smooth. Bring to a boil, reduce the heat, and simmer.
3. Meanwhile, melt the remaining tablespoon of butter in a sauté pan. Add the shallots and cook for 2 minutes. Add the sliced mushrooms and sauté over medium heat for 4 to 5 minutes.
4. Add the dry cider or white wine and reduce over high heat for 4 to 5 minutes.
5. Combine the 2 mixtures and simmer for 10 to 15 minutes more.
6. Stir in the heavy cream or crème fraîche, bring to a boil, and reduce for 5 minutes at a steady boil. Remove from the heat and season to taste.

FISH VELOUTÉ
Thickened and Enriched Fish Stock

A very basic sauce, this is usually only a foundation from which to build richer, more complex sauces. However, if the fish stock you are using is flavorful enough, there is no reason why this cannot be served with most fish or seafood.

YIELD: 2 CUPS

2 tablespoons butter
2 teaspoons chopped
  shallots

3 tablespoons flour
2 cups Fish Stock (page 30)
Salt and white pepper

1. Melt the butter in a medium saucepan. Add the shallots and cook for a minute or two over medium heat.
2. Stir the flour vigorously into the butter and shallots and cook for 3 or 4 minutes. The flour should remain pale blond in color.
3. Add the stock and whisk quickly until all the lumps are gone. Bring to a boil, reduce the heat, and simmer for 30 minutes.
4. Strain the velouté to remove the shallots. Season to taste.

SAUCE NORMANDE POUR POISSONS
Cream Sauce for Fish

An excellent way to vary fish velouté is to add chopped fresh herbs such as parsley, tarragon, chervil, or chives. Or try adding chopped steamed oysters. This is wonderful over salmon, cod, scallops, or nearly any baked or boiled fish.

2 tablespoons butter
1 teaspoon chopped shallots
1 cup sliced mushrooms
1 cup Fish Velouté (page
    34)
1 cup heavy cream or
    Crème Fraîche (page
    23)

1 egg yolk
Few drops of lemon juice
Salt and pepper

YIELD: 2½ CUPS

1. Melt the butter in a medium saucepan over medium heat. Add the shallots, cover, and cook for a few minutes.
2. Add the mushrooms, cover, and cook over low heat for about 5 minutes.
3. Add the fish velouté. Bring the mixture just to a boil, reduce the heat, and simmer very gently for 15 to 20 minutes, stirring occasionally.
4. In a separate bowl mix the heavy cream or crème fraîche with the egg yolk. Very slowly, stir a little of the fish velouté into the cream-and-egg mixture to raise the temperature. Then stir the cream mixture back into the fish velouté. Let it just come to a boil—1 or 2 bubbles—and remove from the heat.
5. Squeeze a few drops of lemon juice into the sauce. Season to taste.

SAUCE À LA CRÈME POUR LÉGUMES
Cream Sauce for Vegetables

Without the addition of meat or fish essences of some kind, a cream sauce does not qualify to be called a sauce normande in Normandy. Nonetheless, this airy sauce perfectly complements gently poached or steamed vegetables such as cauliflower or broccoli. If you happen to end up with some left over, reheat the sauce and serve it for breakfast over soft-boiled eggs.

YIELD: 3 CUPS

2 tablespoons butter
2 teaspoons chopped onions
3 tablespoons flour
2 cups milk

1 cup Crème Fraîche (page
　23)
⅛ teaspoon nutmeg
Salt and white pepper

1. Melt the butter in a medium saucepan. Add the onions and cook over medium heat for 2 to 3 minutes. Stir in the flour and cook for another 2 or 3 minutes.

2. Add 1 cup of the milk and bring the mixture to a boil, stirring constantly. Add the remaining cup milk and bring back to a boil, still stirring. Reduce the heat and simmer for 15 minutes, stirring occasionally.

3. Add the crème fraîche, bring to a boil, and remove from the heat. Add the nutmeg and season to taste.

VINAIGRE DE CIDRE
Cider Vinegar

A good homemade cider vinegar requires only two ingredients and a little attention. In fact, this recipe should make demands only on your patience. However, if you save the *mère,* or starter, from the first recipe and add it to each subsequent mixture, the 12-week fermentation process can be reduced to 9 weeks, and you'll end up with a vinegar of an even finer quality.

To vary the taste of the vinegar, you may wish to add nuts or berries after the second fermentation. For each quart of vinegar, add 1 cup of strawberries or raspberries and let the fruit macerate for about 3 weeks before using. The same amount of blueberries should macerate for up to 2 months.

Hazlenuts and walnuts are also excellent. For each quart of vinegar add 2 dozen unshelled hazelnuts or shelled walnuts. Let the nuts macerate in the vinegar for up to 2 months and then use as needed.

1 teaspoon honey   *3 quarts sweet cider,*   YIELD: 2
                                      unpasteurized   QUARTS

1. Dissolve the honey in the cider in a 1-gallon jar.
2. Cover the jar with a piece of cheesecloth folded in half and secured to the rim with a rubber band or a string.
3. Let the cider ferment undisturbed for 6 weeks. During this time a foam will form on the surface.
4. At the end of the 6 weeks, strain the mixture through a doubled or tripled cheesecloth into a clean jar, cover again with fresh cheesecloth, and let it ferment for another 6 weeks at room temperature.
5. After 4 to 5 weeks a film will begin to form on the surface. This is the *mère,* or starter.
6. At the end of the second 6-week period, strain the vinegar through a fine filter or 2 or 3 layers of cheesecloth. Save the starter for the next time you make vinegar. It should be added just prior to the second fermentation. This will reduce the waiting time by 3 weeks and yield a superior vinegar. Between uses the starter should be stored in a jar with a little vinegar in the refrigerator.
7. If you wish to flavor the vinegar with nuts or berries, add after the second straining.

Appetizers

When I was growing up, I was convinced that the charcu-tiers or pork butchers of Saint-Hilaire-du-Harcouet were in league together. There must have been seven or eight of them located at strategic intervals across town, their windows always crowded with fresh pâtés and terrines, galantines, bal-lotines, little pots of rillettes and dozens of local sausages. I could usually walk by one shop without faltering, and a con-scious act of will would generally propel me by a second. By the third, however, the window passed more slowly, and by the fourth I was counting up the change in my pockets with serious intent.

Without question charcuterie dishes are the most popular appetizers in Normandy. Probably introduced by the Romans, the art of charcuterie spread throughout the province until few areas cannot claim a local pâté or sausage. Today profes-sional and domestic cooks alike carefully learn to balance the ingredients, ensuring that the finished product will be neither too dry nor too fatty and that the flavor will stimulate the appetite rather than overpower it.

I have included what I think is a fairly representative cross-section of charcuterie dishes in this chapter, with an em-phasis on the simpler, more rustic versions of the recipes. The two boudin recipes I prepared with my mother when I was younger, along with the Pâté de Campagne and Rillettes du Normand. The Terrine de Lièvre is from my days as an ap-prentice chef and is one of the finest and simplest recipes for this dish that I have tried. I selected the Boudin l'Avran-chinaisse because the fish and sweetbreads were such a rare and natural complement.

Unfortunately I have had to omit one of the more notable sausages of the province, Andouilles de Vire, because the laws of the United States prohibit the use of pork intestines in cook-ing. The flavor given to the sausage is so distinctive that I would not even attempt to recommend a substitute.

The appetizers of the province are not limited to just charcuterie, however. There are Diablotins du Camembert —squares of Camembert cheese, breaded and deep-fried; Chaussons aux Crevettes—half-moons of puff pastry filled with shrimp, mushrooms, and a Calvados-laced cream sauce; and

Pommes Farcies du Cotentin—apples filled with cooked meat and moistened with sauce.

Also common as hot appetizers in Normandy are frogs' legs, or cuisses de grenouilles. I have included two variations here—Grenouilles Fermière, frogs' legs sautéed in butter and then cooked in a cream sauce, and Grenouilles à la Mode de Boulay, breaded frogs' legs flavored with garlic, shallots, and parsley.

PÂTÉ DE CAMPAGNE
Pork Pâté

This is an extremely simple pâté to prepare and one which would probably be served in most Norman homes. The ground pâté spice can be purchased at specialty or gourmet stores, or you can make it yourself. Combine roughly equal amounts of ground bay leaf, thyme, nutmeg, and powdered ginger. Once you have experimented with the spice, you may want to alter that ratio to suit your taste. For best results prepare the pâté a day or two before you need it and let it "rest" in the refrigerator. This will bring out all the flavor.

SERVES 10 TO 12

1 pound lean pork shoulder, cubed
½ pound pork liver, coarsely chopped
½ pound pork fatback, cubed
4 tablespoons butter
½ cup finely chopped onions
1 tablespoon Calvados

1½ tablespoons salt
¼ teaspoon pepper
¼ teaspoon Pâté Spice (see above)
6 ounces fatback 4 inches wide by 12 inches long, cut into 4 strips ¹⁄₁₆ to ⅛ inches thick

1. In a food processor coarsely grind the cubed pork shoulder, liver, and fatback in small, workable batches. Transfer to a large mixing bowl.

2. Melt the butter in a saucepan. Add the onions and sauté slowly until they are transparent. Cool, then add to the meat and fat mixture.

3. Add all the other ingredients except the fatback strips. Mix the ingredients for 5 to 10 minutes, or until very well combined.

4. Line a 10- by 4- by 3-inch-high pâté mold with three strips of fatback—one along the bottom and one along either side. Spoon in the meat mixture and even off the top with a spoon. Cover the mixture with the remaining fatback strip. Refrigerate overnight; this will enhance and heighten the flavor.

5. Place the mold in a pan with approximately 1 inch of water in the bottom and bake in a preheated 350°F oven for 1 hour and 45 minutes. Remove and cool.

6. Once cooled, place the mold in a hot water bath for 15 seconds. Invert on a platter and remove the pâté from the mold. Cut into ¼-inch slices.

NOTE   *This pâté will keep for 8 to 10 days in your refrigerator.*

TERRINE DE CANARD À LA ROUENNAISE
Duck Terrine, Rouen Style

Duck is extremely popular in Normandy, and this terrine is traditionally made with Rouennais duckling (see note on page 143). However, if this is not available, you may substitute a Moscovy or even a white Pekin duck.

1 duckling, approximately 5 pounds
½ pound lean pork shoulder, diced into 1-inch cubes, or ½ pound ground pork
1 pound fatback, diced into 1-inch cubes
3 ounces duck or chicken livers, washed and devined
¼ pound ground veal
1 tablespoon butter
¼ cup minced onions
2 teaspoons salt
¼ teaspoon pepper
¼ teaspoon Pâté Spice (see Pâté de Campagne, page 41)
2 teaspoons Calvados
1 egg
½ pound fatback 4 inches wide by 12 inches long, sliced into 5 to 6 strips 1/16 to ⅛ inch thick

SERVES 10 TO 12

1. Remove all duck meat from the carcass, reserving all fat and skin. In a food processor fitted with a metal blade, grind in small batches the duck meat, fat, and skin, pork shoulder, pork fatback, and livers. Add the ground veal and mix well.
2. Melt the butter in a saucepan and sauté the onions until pale yellow. Cool and add to the meat mixture. Add the salt, pepper, pâté spice, Calvados, and egg. Mix well by hand for 5 minutes.
3. Line the bottom and sides of a 2-quart terrine or baking dish with 3 to 4 strips of the fatback. Mound the meat into the center of the dish and cover completely with the remaining fatback strips. The ends of the fatback may overlap.
4. Slide your finger around the inside surface of the dish so that the fatback is not touching the sides. Let the terrine rest in the refrigerator for 3 or 4 hours or overnight if possible.

5. Preheat the oven to 350°F. Place the terrine in a baking pan with about ½ to 1 inch of water in the bottom. Bake covered for 2 hours and 30 minutes. When you remove the terrine from the oven, let it come to room temperature before refrigerating. Serve cold with cornichons or potato salad.

TERRINE DE LIÈVRE
Hare Terrine

Full-grown Norman hares weigh about 12 to 15 pounds, and only the front half of the animal is used to make pâtés or terrines. The rest of the meat is often braised or used in stews. You will get the best results from this dish if you allow it to rest overnight in the refrigerator prior to cooking. The ingredients will blend and the overall flavor will be mellower.

SERVES 12

1 pound wild or domestic rabbit meat, fresh or frozen, boned and diced into 1-inch cubes
1 pound lean pork shoulder, diced into 1-inch cubes
½ pound fresh fatback, diced into 1-inch cubes
1 clove garlic, finely minced
2 tablespoons finely chopped shallots

2 tablespoons Calvados or brandy
¼ teaspoon Pâté Spice (see Pâté de Campagne, page 41)
1 tablespoon salt
½ teaspoon pepper
½ pound fatback 4 inches wide by 12 inches long, sliced into 5 to 6 strips ¹⁄₁₆ to ⅛ inch thick

1. Place the cubed rabbit, pork, and fatback in a large bowl with the garlic, shallots, and Calvados. Mix then marinate for 3 to 4 hours.
2. Remove the meat, reserving any marinade. In a food processor fitted with a metal blade, grind the rabbit, pork, and

fatback in small batches. Mix the reserved marinade back into the ground meats.

3. To the ground meat mixture add the pâté spice, salt, and pepper and mix well by hand for about 5 minutes.

4. Line the bottom and sides of a 2-quart terrine or baking dish with 3 to 4 strips of the fatback. Mound the meat into the center of the dish and cover completely with remaining fatback strips. The ends of the fatback may overlap.

5. Slide your finger completely around the inside surface of the dish so that the fatback is not touching the sides. Let the terrine rest in the refrigerator overnight.

6. Preheat the oven to 350°F. Place the terrine in a baking pan with about ½ to 1 inch of water in the bottom. Cover the pan (aluminum foil over the top is acceptable) and bake for 1 hour. Remove the cover and cook for another 45 minutes.

7. Remove, cool, and serve in slices.

NOTE

This terrine is often served with a gelée or an aspic coating. It is not necessary, but if you wish to try it, here is the recipe. Blanch ½ pound pork skin and 1 calf's foot for about 5 minutes in boiling water. Remove, wash well, and discard the water. Place the skin and foot in a large pot, add 2 quarts water, and bring to a boil. Add 1 medium onion, peeled and halved, with 1 clove stuck in each half, and 1 tablespoon salt. Reduce the heat and simmer for 3 hours. Remove the foot, skin, and onion halves and strain the liquid. This must be poured over the terrine while both are still hot. Cool and serve sliced.

RILLETTES DU NORMAND
Potted Pork

There is no simpler charcuterie item to prepare than rillettes. Traditionally, the cooked pork was shredded with two forks or pounded in a mortar, and when I was an apprentice chef, we even pushed the meat through a sieve. However, there is no reason that this task cannot be updated by using a food processor. Serve as a dip with fresh vegetables or as a spread at parties with French bread.

YIELD: 3 TO 4 CUPS

1 pound pork shoulder, cut into 1-inch cubes
½ pound pork fatback, cut into 1-inch cubes
Bouquet garni (1 bay leaf, 1 sprig fresh thyme, 4 green leek leaves, and 10 to 12 stems parsley tied together or in a cheesecloth bag)

1 small onion, peeled, halved, and studded with 1 clove in each half
Salt and pepper

1. Cover the cubed pork shoulder and fatback with approximately 1 quart water. Bring to a boil, then reduce the heat. Add the bouquet garni and the 2 onion halves. Simmer for 2½ to 3 hours. The meat must be cooked until it is virtually falling apart.

2. Remove and discard the onion and the bouquet garni. Remove the meat, reserving the liquid and the fat. Place the meat in a food processor fitted with the metal blade and shred it; you do not want to purée the meat.

3. Meanwhile, reduce the liquid in the pot over medium heat for 20 to 30 minutes, or until the fat becomes transparent. In essence, you will be boiling off most of the water and clarifying the fat.

4. Cool the fat a little, then add the shredded meat back into it. Mix well. Refrigerate for 24 hours. Season to taste, and serve chilled.

NOTE   *Rillettes will keep for 8 to 10 days in your refrigerator.*

RAMEQUINS DE FOIE AU CALVADOS
Individual Chicken Liver Pâtés Laced with Calvados

1 pound chicken livers,
    washed and devined
6 eggs
¼ cup flour
1 cup heavy cream
8 tablespoons butter,
    melted

2 tablespoons Calvados
¼ teaspoon Pâté Spice (see
    Pâté de Campagne,
    page 41)
1 clove garlic, crushed
2 teaspoons salt

1. In food processor fitted with a metal blade or a blender, purée the chicken livers.
2. Add the remaining ingredients and continue to purée until the mixture is smooth, approximately 5 minutes.
3. Divide the chicken liver mixture among the ramekins, filling each to within ¼ inch of the rim.
4. Place the ramekins in a pan with approximately ½ inch of water in the bottom and bake in a preheated 300°F oven for 1 hour and 15 minutes.
5. Remove and cool. This dish is at its best when served at room temperature, so if you refrigerate the pâté, remove the ramekins from the refrigerator about an hour before serving.

Use eight 4-ounce ramekins or soufflé molds.

SERVES 8

BOUDIN À L'AVRANCHINAISSE
Poached Pike and Sweetbreads in a Creamy Fish Broth

This is an old recipe that originated around the town of Avranches, not far from the Abbey of Mont-Saint-Michel. Although it is rarely prepared any more, you still may find it offered in a few local restaurants or inns when fresh pike is available.

SERVES 8

Sauce

2 tablespoons butter
2 tablespoons flour
2 cups Fish Stock (page 30)

1 cup heavy cream
¼ teaspoon lemon juice
Salt and white pepper

Boudin

1 pound pike (if not available, sole, bass, or tilefish may be substituted)
4 egg yolks

1 teaspoon salt
¼ teaspoon white pepper
1 cup fresh bread crumbs
1½ cups heavy cream
½ pound sweetbreads

1. To make the sauce, melt the butter in a medium saucepan. Add the flour and stir over medium heat for 2 to 3 minutes.
2. Gradually stir in the fish stock so it will not form lumps. Bring to a boil, reduce the heat, and simmer for 15 minutes.
3. Add the heavy cream, lemon juice, and salt and pepper to taste. Keep warm on low heat or the back of the stove.
4. To make the boudin, place the fish and egg yolks in a food processor and purée.
5. Add the salt, white pepper, bread crumbs, and approximately ⅓ of the cream. Combine until smooth in the food processor.
6. Add the next ⅓ of the cream. Process. Add the remaining cream and process. The mixture should have a smooth texture. Transfer the mixture to a bowl and refrigerate for about 30 minutes.
7. Place the sweetbreads in 1 quart water, bring to a boil, quickly reduce the heat, and simmer for 15 minutes.

8. Remove the sweetbreads and plunge them into cold water. Leave them there until cool. Under cold running water completely remove all membranes, connective tubes, and fat. Dice the sweetbreads into ¼-inch cubes. Fold them into the fish mixture and refrigerate again for 30 minutes more.

9. Take approximately 3 ounces or ½ cup of the fish and sweetbreads mixture and roll it into a sausage about 3 inches long by ¾ inch in diameter. You may sprinkle the board with a little flour to make the sausages easier to roll, but use it sparingly. Continue to roll until all the mixture has been used; it should yield 16 sausages.

10. Meanwhile, in a large pot bring 1 gallon water to a boil, reduce the heat, and simmer. Place 6 boudin at a time into the water and poach for 8 to 10 minutes. Drain and transfer to an ovenproof baking dish. When all the boudin are in the dish, add the sauce, cover the dish, and place in a preheated 350°F oven for about 30 minutes. The boudin should puff slightly. Remove from the oven and serve immediately.

BOUDIN NOIR AU CERFEUIL
Blood Pudding Sausage
Flavored with Chervil

Everyone has a favorite recipe for boudin noir, and I have seen it made in Normandy with diced apples, chestnuts, and even crème fraîche. The following recipe is a little more basic, however, and one which I have prepared at home dozens of times. Both the boudin noir and the boudin blanc are traditional holiday dishes in the province, and they are usually served on Christmas Eve with sautéed apples and mashed potatoes—a dish called Boudin avec Deux Pommes.

Both boudin noir and boudin blanc should not be kept for   NOTE
more than 3 or 4 days refrigerated. However, boudin blanc can
be frozen for 1 or 2 months if wrapped tightly in plastic wrap.

SERVES 6 TO 8

*¾ pound fatback, cut into
    4 pieces
4 cups fresh pork blood (if
    not available, use beef
    blood)
1 tablespoon finely chopped
    chervil*

*2 teaspoons salt
¼ teaspoon pepper
¼ teaspoon Pâté Spice (see
    Pâté de Campagne,
    page 41)
1 yard sausage casing*

NOTE   *Both the blood and sausage casing should be available from
your butcher or a specialty store.*

1. Place the pork fatback in a pot with 8 cups water. Bring to a boil and continue to boil for 20 minutes. Drain in a colander. Allow the fat to cool, then dice into ⅛-inch cubes.

2. In a bowl mix the fatback with the blood. Add the chopped chervil, salt, pepper, and pâté spice. Stir well.

3. Wash the sausage casing well inside and out with cold water. Make a knot at one end and tie it off with a piece of string.

4. Fit the nozzle of a sausage funnel into the open end of the casing and gradually fill with the blood and fatback mixture. Fill the casing to 2 inches from the top. Twist, make a knot with the casing, and tie it off with a piece of string.

5. Place the sausage in a large pot containing 1 gallon of water. Heat the water to 160°F—no bubbles should break the surface of the water—and poach for 15 minutes, occasionally stirring gently with a wooden spoon to maintain an even temperature.

6. Take a very sharp needle and gently prick any area where large air pockets have formed. This will prevent the casing from popping.

7. Poach for 15 minutes more. Pierce the boudin with the needle. If no blood runs out, the sausage is cooked and should be removed from the water; if the blood is still liquid, poach for a few minutes more.

8. Cool the boudin completely. With a sharp knife, cut it in 4- to 6-inch sections. Place under a hot broiler for a few minutes or sauté in butter until heated through. Boudin is served hot.

To serve Boudin avec Deux Pommes, core and slice Granny Smith apples, allowing ½ apple for each person. Melt 1 to 2 tablespoons of butter in a skillet and sauté slices of boudin noir for 1 to 2 minutes. Add the sliced apples and sauté for 3 to 4 minutes more, or until apples begin to brown. Serve boudin and apple slices with mashed potatoes. You can also replace the boudin noir with boudin blanc (see the next recipe).

BOUDIN BLANC
White Pudding Sausage

Like boudin noir, this sausage is served hot, as an appetizer or as a light supper entrée.

1 cup milk
4 cups French bread, crusts
*   removed and sliced*
*   into ½-inch cubes*
½ pound lean pork butt
¼ pound fresh fatback
2 eggs, beaten

1 teaspoon salt
¼ teaspoon white pepper
1 teaspoon Calvados
⅛ teaspoon nutmeg
⅛ teaspoon ground cloves
1 yard sausage casing

SERVES 6 TO 8

If you purchase the pork butt and fat back from your butcher, ask him to grind both of them on a "fine" or "small" dial setting. This will save you a step later. Sausage casing should be available from your butcher or a specialty store.

NOTE

1. Bring the milk to a boil in a saucepan. Pour it over the diced bread in a large bowl. Let the bread soak for 30 minutes.
2. If the pork butt and fatback are not already ground, cut them into 1-inch cubes. Grind in small batches in a food processor.
3. Once the milk and bread mixture is cool, add the ground pork and fatback. Add the beaten eggs, salt, pepper, Calvados,

nutmeg, and ground cloves. Mix well. The consistency should be very loose, almost runny.

4. Wash the sausage casing well inside and out with cold water. Make a knot at one end and tie it off with a piece of string.

5. Fit the nozzle of a sausage funnel into the open end of the casing and gently work in the mixture. If you roll up the casing, letting it out gradually as it fills, this process will be a little less unwieldy. If the mixture clogs in the funnel, push it through with the round handle of a kitchen utensil, possibly a small wooden spoon.

6. Twist the casing every 4 inches and tie off with string to make separate boudin. Repeat the process until all the mixture is used.

7. Place the sausage in a large pot containing 1 gallon water. Heat the water to 160°F—no bubbles should break the surface of the water—and poach for about 20 minutes, stirring occasionally gently with a wooden spoon to maintain an even temperature.

8. Prick the boudin with a needle after 20 minutes. If the liquid comes out clear, the sausages are cooked. Remove from the water and cool.

9. When cool, separate sausages by cutting at the twists with a sharp knife. To serve, cook in a little butter or place under the broiler for approximately 10 minutes.

GRENOUILLES FERMIÈRE
Frogs' Legs, Farmer Style

Frogs' legs, with their sweet, delicate flavor, make wonderful summer appetizers. In Normandy our source was a small pond at one end of the farm where we took the cows everyday to drink. The pond banks were thick with watercress, a favorite sanctuary for the frogs, and my brothers and I never had any problems capturing enough of them for the entire family.

I have included two recipes, both of which are quite tasty as well as easy to prepare. The first, Grenouilles Fermière, is a fairly well-known preparation throughout the province, while the second, which originates in the town of Boulay, is not as common. Your local fish store should be able to order frogs' legs.

24 medium frogs' legs
1 cup milk
½ cup flour
4 tablespoons butter
Salt and pepper

⅔ cup heavy cream or
*   Crème Fraîche (page 23)*
1 teaspoon cider vinegar
1 tablespoon finely chopped
*   chives*

SERVES 4

1. Wash the frogs' legs in cold water and dry well. Cut them in half at the joint and soak in the milk for approximately 5 minutes. Remove and shake off excess milk.
2. Flour lightly, shaking off excess.
3. Melt the butter in a skillet and add the floured frogs' legs in small batches, browning lightly on both sides. Transfer them to an ovenproof platter.
4. Season the legs with salt and pepper and pour the heavy cream over them. Place the platter in a preheated 400°F oven until the cream reduces somewhat and the legs have browned a little more.
5. Remove the platter from the oven and sprinkle the frogs' legs with the cider vinegar and the chopped chives. Serve at once.

GRENOUILLES
À LA MODE DE BOULAY
Frogs' Legs Flavored with Garlic, Parsley, and Shallots

SERVES 4

24 medium frogs' legs
2 cups dry bread crumbs
1 clove garlic, finely
 chopped
½ cup finely chopped fresh
 parsley
2 teaspoons finely chopped
 shallots

1 teaspoon salt
¼ teaspoon pepper
8 tablespoons butter,
 melted
1½ tablespoons lemon juice

1. Wash the frogs' legs in cold water and dry well. Cut them in half at the joint.
2. Combine the bread crumbs, chopped garlic, parsley, shallots, salt, and pepper. Mix well.
3. Dip the frogs' legs into the melted butter, coating well on both sides.
4. Dredge the coated frogs' legs in the bread-crumb mixture, pressing the crumbs with your hand so they adhere to the legs better.
5. Place the frogs' legs on a lightly buttered baking dish or an ovenproof platter in a preheated 450°F oven for 15 minutes. Turn them over, reduce the heat to 350°F, and continue to bake for another 15 minutes.
6. Remove the frogs' legs from the oven and sprinkle them with the lemon juice. Serve at once.

FLAN DE MOULES CAENNAISE
Mussel and Cheese Tart

Pâte à Tarte   SERVES 8 TO 10
1½ cups flour
½ teaspoon salt
1½ teaspoons sugar

6 tablespoons butter
1 small egg yolk

Filling
2 dozen small mussels
1½ cups heavy cream or
    half-and-half
4 eggs
⅛ teaspoon nutmeg
1 teaspoon salt

⅛ teaspoon pepper
1¼ cups grated Gruyère or
    French Emmenthaler
    cheese
1 teaspoon butter

1. To make the pie dough, in a large chilled mixing bowl work together the flour, salt, sugar, and butter with your fingertips until it reaches the consistency of sand. Add the egg yolk and blend for 1 minute more. Add 2 tablespoons ice water and lightly toss the mixture with a fork. If the dough is still crumbly, gradually add up to 3 more tablespoons ice water until the dough is workable. Form the dough into a ball and refrigerate in plastic wrap for at least 1 hour, or until it is firm.

2. Scrub the mussels well with a stiff-bristled brush and remove the beards. Place them in a large pot with ½ cup water. Bring to a boil, cover, and steam for 8 to 10 minutes, or until all the mussels have opened. Discard any that have not.

3. Remove the mussels from the pot. The cooking liquor is not used in this recipe, but if you wish to save it, strain it through cheesecloth and refrigerate in a covered bowl.

4. In a large bowl combine the heavy cream, eggs, nutmeg, salt, and pepper and mix well. Add the grated cheese and continue to mix.

5. Remove the pie dough from the refrigerator and place on a floured board or table. Let it rest for a few minutes. Dust a little flour on it, then roll out into a circle approximately ⅛ inch thick by about 12 inches in diameter. Butter the bottom

and sides of a 9- or 10-inch false-bottom quiche pan or pie mold. Place the dough in the pie mold, pressing down along the edges to trim off excess dough. Gently prick the dough with a fork along the bottom.

6. Remove the mussels from their shells and evenly distribute them along the bottom of the shell. Pour the cream, egg, and cheese mixture into the shell. Bake in a preheated 350°F oven for 50 minutes, or until a knife inserted in the center comes out clean.

7. Let the flan rest for approximately 15 minutes before serving.

NOTE *This flan can be made with any leftover cooked fish or shellfish.*

LA FICELLE NORMANDE
Thinly Rolled Pancakes Filled with Ham

Ficelle, or "string" crêpes, are tightly rolled pancakes traditionally about ¼ to ½ inch in diameter, hence the name. This is a very basic recipe, but ficelles can be filled with anything you choose—thinly sliced cooked chicken, scallops, mushrooms, and so on, providing the filling does not swell the pancake too much. Then it simply reverts to being a crêpe.

Pancake Batter (enough for approximately 18 pancakes)   SERVES 6

1 cup flour
½ teaspoon salt
2 eggs
1¼ cups milk

2 tablespoons butter,
   melted
8 tablespoons (1 stick)
   butter, frozen

Filling

1 cup milk
2 tablespoons Beurre Manié
   (page 23)
⅛ teaspoon nutmeg
2 ounces Camembert
   cheese, with rind
   removed and cut into
   small pieces

Salt and white pepper
18 slices smoked ham, cut
   approximately 5 by 5
   by ¹⁄₁₆ inch thick, or as
   thin as possible

Sauce

1 cup Crème Fraîche (page
   23)

2 tablespoons butter
Salt and white pepper

1. To make the pancake batter, mix the flour, salt, and eggs in a large bowl. Add ½ cup of the milk and mix well to avoid lumps. Stir in the melted butter. Add the remaining milk and mix vigorously for a minute or two. This mixture does not have to be refrigerated before using.
2. Set a pan over medium heat—a black steel pan is best, but a crêpe pan or skillet will work—and coat the bottom of the pan by rubbing it with the frozen butter. Ladle enough batter

into the pan to make a pancake approximately 6 inches in diameter and as thin as possible. Cook the pancake until it begins to brown and then flip with a spatula. Cook for approximately 30 seconds more and transfer it to a plate. Place a piece of waxed paper over each pancake as you stack them. If the pancakes begin to stick, add more butter to the pan.

3. To make the filling, bring the milk to a boil in a small saucepan and add the beurre manié, whisking quickly so it does not lump. Add the nutmeg and blend in the Camembert cheese. Simmer for 3 or 4 minutes. Remove from the heat and season to taste.

4. To make the sauce, bring the heavy cream or crème fraîche to a boil, stir in the butter, and season to taste.

5. To assemble the ficelle, place 1 slice ham on each pancake, and then spread approximately 1½ teaspoons of the filling on the ham. Roll the filled pancake as tightly as possible and place in an ovenproof dish. Continue the procedure until all the pancakes have been filled.

6. Pour the sauce over the pancakes and bake in a preheated 400°F oven for 10 minutes.

7. Serve 3 ficelles for each person.

CHAUSSONS AUX CREVETTES
Puff Pastry
Filled with Shrimp, Mushrooms,
and a Calvados-laced Cream Sauce

This is wonderful dish, prepared in Normandy with tiny shrimp called crevettes. Use the smallest shrimp you can find or simply cut larger ones into halves or thirds.

4 tablespoons butter
¾ pound small shrimp, peeled and deveined
1 cup sliced fresh mushrooms
1 teaspoon finely chopped shallots
¼ teaspoon chopped tarragon leaves, fresh or dried
1 teaspoon Calvados
½ cup Fish Stock (page 30)

½ cup heavy cream
Salt and white pepper
10 ounces Puff Pastry Dough (page 24, approximately ⅓ recipe; or purchase frozen), rolled approximately ⅛ inch thick, and cut into 4 6-inch circles
1 egg yolk, beaten

SERVES 4

1. Melt the butter in a medium saucepan. Add the shrimp and cook over medium heat for 3 or 4 minutes.
2. Add the sliced mushrooms and continue to sauté for 5 minutes. Add the shallots and sauté 1 minute more. Add the tarragon and the Calvados.
3. Add the stock, bring to a boil, and cook over medium heat for about 15 minutes, or until it has reduced by approximately ½. Remove the shrimp and mushrooms with a slotted spoon and set aside.
4. Add the heavy cream and continue to reduce over medium heat for another 10 minutes. Season to taste. Remove from the heat until ready to use.
5. Divide the shrimp-and-mushroom mixture equally among the puff pastry circles. Fold the circles in half, sealing with a little egg yolk. Bake on a sheetpan in a preheated 450°F oven for approximately 8 to 10 minutes. To serve, reheat the sauce, pour it onto individual plates, and top with the filled puffs.

RISSOLES DE PERDREAUX
Partridge and Apples in Puff Pastry

We usually used red-legged partridge in this savory dish, but you can use any freshly roasted partridge. If partridge is not available, quail or pheasant make good stand-bys. This is an excellent dish to use up leftover game bird of any kind.

SERVES 4

2 partridges, approximately ¾ pound each
1 tablespoon butter
2 tablespoons finely chopped onions
1 apple (Granny Smith, Golden Delicious, or McIntosh), peeled, cored, and diced into ¼-inch cubes

½ cup cream
Salt and pepper
1 egg yolk
8 ounces Puff Pastry Dough (page 24, approximately ⅙ recipe; or purchase frozen), rolled out and cut into 4- by 4- by ⅛-inch squares

1. Roast unseasoned partridges for approximately 30 minutes in a preheated 350°F oven. Cool and remove all the meat. Dice into ¼-inch cubes.
2. Melt the butter in a saucepan. Add the partridge and the onions and sauté over medium heat for 3 or 4 minutes.
3. Add the diced apple, cream, salt and pepper. Toss gently to coat meat and reduce until mixture thickens. Remove pan from the heat and cool.
4. Mix the egg yolk with a few drops of water in a bowl.
5. Place the meat mixture in the center of each puff pastry square. Make a triangle by folding the top corner over the bottom and seal with a little egg yolk. Then brush the top with the egg yolk.
6. Bake on a sheet pan for 15 to 20 minutes in a preheated 400° F oven. Serve hot.

DIABLOTINS AU CAMEMBERT
Deep-fried Squares of Camembert Cheese

The basic preparation for this dish has its counterpart in nearly every province of France, but the addition of Camembert cheese makes it uniquely Norman. These make excellent hot hors d'oeuvres at parties.

4 tablespoons butter
6 tablespoons flour
2 cups milk
1 clove
⅛ teaspoon nutmeg
¼ pound Camembert
    cheese, with rind
    removed and cut into
    ¼-inch pieces

Salt and white pepper
4 cups peanut oil
2 eggs, beaten
1 cup dry bread crumbs

SERVES 6

1. Melt the butter in a saucepan. Stir in the flour and cook for 2 to 3 minutes.
2. Add the milk to the butter and flour mixture, stirring vigorously so it does not lump. Bring to a boil. Stir in the clove and nutmeg. Reduce the heat and simmer for 5 minutes. Remove the clove.
3. Add the Camembert cheese and mix well. Simmer for 5 minutes more. Stir well. Remove from the heat and season to taste.
4. Pour the mixture into a 9- by 12-inch baking pan and smooth the surface with a spatula. Refrigerate for at least 4 hours, or until thoroughly chilled.
5. When cool, cut the cheese mixture into 1½-inch squares.
6. In a medium saucepan bring the peanut oil to 350°F.
7. Dip each cheese square into the beaten egg and then dredge in the bread crumbs. Repeat this process or the crust will be too thin and the cheese mixture will melt into the oil.
8. Place the squares in the hot oil and deep fry until they turn golden brown. Drain on paper towels and serve immediately.

ARTICHAUDS EN FEUILLE TIÈDE
Artichoke Leaves
in a Cream and Cider Vinegar Sauce

The neighboring province of Brittany produces the fattest, meatiest artichokes in France, but so many of them are sold in Lower Normandy that they have become a part of the province's cuisine.

SERVES 4

4 fresh whole medium artichokes
1 teaspoon lemon juice
2 tablespoons salt
¼ cup cider vinegar
1 teaspoon finely chopped shallots

½ teaspoon salt
Freshly ground pepper
½ teaspoon sugar
¾ cup heavy cream

1. Grip the top of an artichoke firmly and snap off the stem as close to the base as possible. This removes the stringy fibers from the artichoke bottom. Trim the base with a small knife and rub with a little lemon juice to prevent discoloring.
2. Remove the small leaves from around the base of the artichoke—there will be 5 or 6—and trim approximately ½ inch from the tops of all remaining leaves with scissors. Repeat Steps 1 and 2 for each artichoke.
3. Bring 3 quarts water containing 2 tablespoons salt to a boil and slip the artichokes into the water. Bring the water back to a boil, reduce the heat, and simmer for 35 to 40 minutes, or until the leaves are tender and can be removed easily.
4. Remove the artichokes from the water and drain well. Pull the leaves from each artichoke. Keep separated and set aside.
5. Remove the choke from each artichoke heart and trim the bottoms with a small knife. Rub each heart with a little lemon juice again and set aside.
6. In a bowl mix the cider vinegar, chopped shallots, salt, a few grinds of pepper, and sugar. Then gradually whisk in the heavy cream. Divide the mixture among 4 small dishes for dipping

and place them in the center of 4 larger plates. Arrange the artichoke leaves around each dish.

7. Cut each artichoke bottom into 6 pieces and arrange on the plates.

POMMES FARCIES DU COTENTIN
Baked Stuffed Apples

A very popular way to use leftovers, created by some frugal Norman cook. This is excellent with beef, lamb, pork, or veal, but you should also have some of the sauce or gravy from the leftover dish to add flavor.

4 large apples (Granny Smith, Golden Delicious, or McIntosh)
1 cup coarsely chopped leftover beef, lamb, pork, or veal
Salt and pepper
2 teaspoons butter
¼ cup dry bread crumbs
1 cup leftover sauce or gravy

SERVES 4

1. Core the apples without breaking the bottom skin. Slice off the tops and set aside. Scoop out approximately ½ the pulp from each apple.
2. Chop the apple pulp with a knife and mix it with the chopped leftover meat. Place the mixture in a food processor fitted with a metal blade and process for 10 to 15 seconds. Season to taste.
3. Fill the apples, mounding the excess meat and apple mixture on top. Place the apple tops on the mixture. Put about ½ teaspoon of the butter on each apple top and sprinkle with the bread crumbs.
4. Place the apples in a baking dish with the leftover sauce or gravy. Cover and bake in a preheated 375°F oven for approximately 45 minutes. Serve hot.

Soups

*T*he Vikings are said to have been fond of boiled meats and the broths reserved from those dishes, and perhaps this affinity has contributed to the popularity of soup in Norman cooking today. Unlike the Vikings, however, modern Norman cooks concentrate less on meat broths and more on rich soups prepared from fresh fish, shellfish, and vegetables.

Normandy's coastal waters provide a wide variety of superb shellfish, and two of those—coques, tiny, sweet clams the size of a thumbnail, and fat, satiny mussels—are the basis for Soupe aux Coques and Soupe aux Moules, respectively. Velouté Joinville combines crevettes—diminutive shrimp—with mussels and fresh mushrooms in a creamy fish broth.

Farther inland vegetables are the foundation for many of the region's soups. Onions, cabbages, turnips, potatoes, leeks, and pale yellow pumpkins are puréed, chopped, or sliced, simmered in broth, and perhaps served with a garnish of toasted croutons. Even the first green beans of the year are picked for Soupe au Pei de Mai, a Norman specialty served only in the spring. In most cases, the vegetables are cooked in butter, but in a few instances, such as Soup à l'Oignon du Paysan or Soupe aux Choux, the vegetables are cooked in graisse normande.

My father's favorite vegetable soup, Crème de Légumes du Cotentin, was never called by its proper name at home. We just called it garden soup because the recipe would vary from preparation to preparation, depending upon what my mother picked from her kitchen garden that day. It was quite common for lunch or a light supper merely to be freshly made garden soup, bread and butter, a wheel of Camembert or Pont l'Évêque, and a bottle or two of chilled cork cider.

But a real treat during late summer and early fall, when the heat would still be hanging in the air at the end of the day, would be a bowl of La Pommeraie Glacée, a chilled apple soup. Made with Reine de Reinettes apples and enriched with fresh cream and a little Calvados, this very Norman soup could make even the simplest meal memorable.

SOUPE À LA GRAISSE
A Hearty Soup Flavored with Clarified Fats and Vegetable Essences

This is a very old and traditional recipe from the Manche area. It is rarely prepared today. Although the potatoes appear to be the primary ingredient, the dominant flavor in this soup is still the graisse normande. Serve it on a cold winter day for lunch or as the main course of a light dinner.

8 tablespoons Graisse Normande (page 21)
2 to 3 cups onions, halved and thinly sliced
1 clove garlic, finely chopped
5 to 6 cups potatoes, washed, peeled, and thinly sliced
10 cups Chicken Stock (page 29) or water
16 thin slices French bread
Salt and pepper
2 teaspoons chopped chervil (chopped fresh parsley is also acceptable)

SERVES 6 TO 8

1. In a 5- to 6-quart pot melt the graisse normande over medium heat. Add the onions and cook until transparent. Add the garlic and cook a few minutes more.
2. Add the potatoes and the chicken stock or water. Bring to a boil, reduce the heat, and simmer for approximately 1 hour.
3. While the soup is simmering, dry the slices of French bread in a low oven. When dry, place in the bottom of a tureen or serving bowl.
4. Remove the soup from the heat and season to taste before serving. Pour over bread slices.
5. Sprinkle with chopped chervil before serving.

SOUPE AUX CHOUX
Cabbage Soup

This soup may be eaten cold during the summer, like mine-strone. It can also be served with slices of French bread that have been sautéed in a little graisse normande.

SERVES 6 TO 8

2 tablespoons Graisse Normande (page 21) or butter

1 cup onions, peeled and diced in ½-inch cubes

1 pound Savoy cabbage, cored and coarsely chopped into 1-inch squares

1 cup carrots, peeled, sliced in half lengthwise, and cut into ¼-inch slices

1 cup turnips, peeled, sliced in half lengthwise, and cut into ¼-inch slices

8 cups Chicken Stock (page 29)

1 bay leaf

1½ cups potatoes, washed, peeled, and diced into ½-inch cubes

Salt and pepper

1. Melt the graisse normande or butter in a pot. Add the onions and cook for 4 to 5 minutes, or until transparent.
2. Add the cabbage, carrots, and turnips, cover, and cook over medium heat for 10 minutes.
3. Add the stock and the bay leaf, bring to a boil, then add the potatoes. Reduce the heat and simmer for 1 hour and 15 minutes.
4. Season to taste.

CRÈME DE CRESSON
Cream of Watercress Soup

4 cups Chicken Stock (page
  29)
2 cups watercress, washed
  and finely chopped
3 tablespoons butter
3 tablespoons flour

1½ cups Crème Fraîche
  (page 23)
Salt and pepper

SERVES 6

1. In a large saucepan bring the chicken stock to a boil. Add the watercress, reduce the heat, and simmer for 15 to 20 minutes.
2. Drain the watercress in a colander and reserve the stock.
3. In a blender or food processor purée the watercress into a smooth paste.
4. Melt the butter in a saucepan. Stir in the flour and cook for 3 to 4 minutes over medium heat.
5. Gradually stir the stock into the butter-and-flour mixture. Do not let it lump. Bring to a boil, reduce the heat, and simmer for 2 to 3 minutes.
6. Add the puréed watercress and crème fraîche. Remove from the heat and season to taste.

SOUPE À L'OIGNON DU PAYSAN
Onion Soup, Norman Style

I never knew there was any other way of making onion soup before I left home to become an apprentice to a chef. The graisse normande and the Calvados give the soup a distinctly Norman flavor that I miss when I eat onion soup anywhere else. Naturally, the graisse normande is optional—although I recommend you try the recipe with it once—as is the toasted French bread and melted cheese.

SERVES 6

8 tablespoons Graisse
    Normande (page 21) or
    butter
2 ½ to 3 cups sliced onions
4 tablespoons flour
8 cups Chicken Stock (page
    29)
2 tablespoons Calvados
    (optional)

1½ cups grated Gruyère or
    French Emmenthaler
    cheese (optional)
12 slices French bread,
    toasted (optional)
Salt and pepper

1. Melt the graisse normande or the butter in a pot. Add the sliced onions, cover, and cook over low heat for approximately 25 minutes, or until the onions begin to color slightly. Stir often so they do not stick to the bottom of the pan.
2. Add the flour and mix well. Cook for 2 or 3 minutes more. Add the chicken stock and bring to a boil. Reduce the heat and simmer for 30 minutes.
3. Add the Calvados 2 to 3 minutes before the soup is finished cooking and season to taste.
4. If you decide to serve this soup gratinée, ladle it out into individual bowls. Float 2 slices of toasted French bread on each and cover with grated cheese. Place the bowls the under broiler until the cheese melts and begins to brown on top.

SOUPE À L'OSEILLE
Puree of Sorrel and Potatoes

Sorrel, also known as "sour grass," grows wild in the meadows around my parents' farm, and we would pick it fresh for soup.

SERVES 4 TO 6

6 tablespoons butter
2 cups sorrel, washed
    thoroughly, ribs
    removed, and coarsely
    chopped
½ cup sliced onions

4 cups Chicken Stock (page
    29)
1½ cups potatoes, washed,
    peeled, and coarsely
    chopped
Salt and pepper

1. Melt the butter in a heavy saucepan. Add the chopped sorrel leaves and cook until they turn dark green.
2. Add the sliced onions and cook for 2 to 3 minutes, stirring well.
3. Pour in the stock and bring to a boil. Add the chopped potatoes, cover, and simmer for approximately 40 minutes.
4. Remove the soup from the heat and purée in a blender, food mill, or food processor.
5. Season to taste.

SOUPE AU PEI DE MAI
Soup Made
with the First Green Beans of the Year

Like the first bottles of Beaujolais Nouveau, this soup is eagerly awaited in parts of Normandy, with the early green beans unofficially signaling the start of a new growing season. Choose small, tender green beans at the store; they will be sweeter and more delicate.

4 tablespoons butter
3 small leeks, washed and
  thinly sliced
1 pound green beans,
  washed, trimmed, and
  cut into ½-inch
  lengths
1 cup potatoes, washed,
  peeled, and diced into
  ¼-inch cubes

¼ cup parsnips, peeled and
  diced into ¼-inch
  cubes
½ cup Crème Fraîche (page
  23)
Salt and pepper

SERVES 6

1. Melt the butter in a pot. Add the leeks, cover, and cook over low heat for 8 to 10 minutes.
2. Add the green beans, 6 cups water, potatoes, and parsnips. Bring to a boil, reduce the heat, and simmer for 40 minutes.
3. Add the crème fraîche and return to a boil. Remove from the heat and season to taste.

LA POMMERAIE GLACÉE
Chilled Apple Soup

This is a marvelous soup for a warm day and not as sweet as you might first imagine. If possible, use Granny Smith apples, although Golden Delicious or McIntosh are also fine.

6 tablespoons butter
2 leeks (white part only), washed and coarsely sliced
5 cups apples, peeled, cored, and diced into ¼-inch cubes
6 cups Chicken Stock (page 29)
1½ to 2 cups potatoes, washed, peeled, and diced into ¼-inch cubes, approximately

1 cup heavy cream
2 teaspoons Calvados (optional)
⅛ teaspoon cinnamon
Salt and pepper
2 apples, peeled, cored, and diced into ¼-inch cubes

SERVES 4 TO 6

1. Melt 4 tablespoons of the butter in a pot. Add the sliced leeks, cover, and cook over medium heat for 3 to 4 minutes.
2. Add the 5 cups of apples and cook uncovered for 5 minutes more.
3. Add the stock and the potatoes. Bring to a boil, reduce the heat, and simmer for 45 minutes.
4. When the soup is finished, purée it in batches in a blender or a food processor until smooth.
5. Stir in the heavy cream, Calvados, and cinnamon. Season to taste. Refrigerate for at least 3 hours, or until cool.
6. Just prior to serving, melt the remaining 2 tablespoons of butter in a skillet. Add the 2 diced apples and sauté lightly for 5 minutes, or until the pulp begins to soften. Drain on paper towels.
7. Garnish the chilled apple soup with the sautéed apples.

SOUPE DE POTIRON
Pumpkin Soup

This is a very simple and basic recipe for a soup that is extremely popular in the south of Normandy. Garnish with croutons that have been oven-dried and then sautéed in butter.

SERVES 4 TO 6

2 to 3 pounds pumpkin,
   seeded, skinned, and
   diced into 1-inch cubes
1 teaspoon salt
2 cups milk

⅛ teaspoon nutmeg
⅛ teaspoon ground cloves
4 tablespoons butter
¼ teaspoon white pepper

1. Place the diced pumpkin in a large pot with 5 to 6 cups water and the salt. Bring to a boil, reduce the heat to medium, and simmer covered for 45 minutes.
2. Drain the pumpkin in a fine colander, then purée it in small batches in a food mill, blender, or food processor.
3. Bring the milk to a boil in a large pot. Stir in the pumpkin purée, nutmeg, cloves, butter, and white pepper.

CRÈME DE LÉGUMES DU COTENTIN
Purée of Vegetable Soup

This soup is an unadorned and hearty dish. The "crème" in the title implies the texture of the soup, although some recipes call for the addition of cream or crème fraîche. If you wish, stir in a cupful of either just prior to serving, or add to any leftover soup the following day to refresh it.

6 tablespoons butter
2 cups coarsely chopped
    leeks (white part
    mostly)
2 cloves garlic, chopped
2 tablespoons chopped
    fresh parsley

3 cups carrots, peeled and
    coarsely chopped
2 cups turnips, peeled and
    coarsely chopped
3 cups potatoes, peeled and
    diced
Salt and pepper

SERVES 6 TO 8

1. In a heavy pot melt 4 tablespoons of the butter. Add the leeks, garlic, and parsley, cover, and cook over low heat for about 5 minutes.
2. Stir in the carrots and turnips, cover, and cook for 5 minutes more.
3. Pour in 3 quarts water and bring to a boil.
4. Add the potatoes, reduce the heat, cover, and let the soup simmer gently for about 45 minutes.
5. Remove the soup from the heat and remove the vegetables with a slotted spoon, reserving the cooking broth. Purée the vegetables in a food processor, blender, or food mill.
6. Stir the purée back into the broth, return to the heat, and bring to a boil. Remove from the heat, whisk in the remaining butter, and season to taste.

BOUILLON DE POULES AUX FLUTES
Norman Chicken and Vegetable Soup

We used petit pois or tiny garden peas in this soup, but fresh peas of any kind will work equally well.

SERVES 4

2 medium carrots, peeled and sliced into ¼-inch rounds

2 medium turnips, peeled and sliced into ¼-inch rounds

2 medium leeks, washed and cut into ½-inch lengths

2 ribs celery, washed and cut into ¼-inch lengths

4 tablespoons butter

4 cups Chicken Stock (page 29)

¼ cup petit pois or fresh peas

Salt and pepper

1. Prepare the carrots, turnips, leeks, and celery but keep them separate.
2. Melt the butter in a heavy pot. Add the leeks and celery, cover, and cook over low heat for 5 minutes.
3. Add the sliced carrots and turnips and cook uncovered for 5 minutes more.
4. Add the stock, bring to a boil, reduce the heat, and simmer for 30 minutes.
5. Add the peas and continue to simmer for another 5 minutes. Season to taste.

NOTE *This soup can also be served with toasted slices of French bread.*

SOUPE AUX MOULES
Creamy Mussel Soup

Normandy is celebrated for its plump, tender mussels, and this soup has been a favorite with Norman fishermen for generations.

3 dozen mussels
1 cup dry white wine (Muscadet or Vouvray, if available)
2 tablespoons finely chopped onions
4 tablespoons butter
3 tablespoons flour

3 cups Fish Stock (see page 30)
⅛ teaspoon saffron
3 tablespoons finely chopped celery
2 egg yolks
1 cup heavy cream
Salt and white pepper

SERVES 4 TO 6

1. Scrub the mussels well with a stiff-bristled brush and remove the beards. Place them in a large pot with the white wine and onions. Bring to a boil, cover, and steam for 8 to 10 minutes, or until all the mussels have opened. Discard any that have not.
2. Remove the mussels from the pot and strain the cooking liquid through cheesecloth. Reserve the liquid and add it to the stock.
3. Melt the butter in a medium saucepan. Add the flour and stir over medium heat for 3 to 4 minutes. Add the fish stock and cooking liquid. Stir well as it comes to a boil. Add the saffron and the celery and simmer, uncovered, for 30 minutes.
4. While the soup is cooking, shell the mussels and set them aside. Combine the eggs yolks and heavy cream.
5. At the end of the 30 minutes, remove the soup from the heat and add the mussels. Then vigorously stir in the egg yolk and cream mixture.
6. Season to taste.

SOUPE AUX COQUES
Clam, Leek, and Carrot Soup Enriched with Crème Fraîche

This creamy clam broth is similar to our New England chowder.

SERVES 4

3 to 4 dozen coques or little neck clams (or the smallest clams available)
4 tablespoons butter
4 tablespoons flour
3 cups Chicken Stock (page 29)
½ cup leeks (white and green parts), sliced into strips 1 by ⅛ by ⅛ inch thick

½ cup carrots, sliced into strips 1 by ⅛ by ⅛ inch thick
½ cup Crème Fraîche (page 23)
1 teaspoon chopped fresh parsley
Salt and white pepper

1. Scrub the clams thoroughly. Place them in a large pot with 1 cup water. Bring to a boil, cover, and steam for 8 to 10 minutes, or until all the clams have opened. Discard any that have not.
2. Remove the clams from the pot. Strain the cooking liquid through cheesecloth and reserve. Shell the clams and keep warm. Reserve the clam juice.
3. Melt the butter in a large pot. Stir in the flour and cook for 2 to 3 minutes over medium heat. Add the chicken stock and all the clam juice, and bring to a boil.
4. Add the leeks and carrots. Reduce the heat and simmer, uncovered, for 20 minutes.
5. Remove from the heat. Add the clams, crème fraîche, and parsley. Season to taste.

VELOUTÉ JOINVILLE
Shrimp, Mussels, and Mushrooms
Cooked in a Rich Fish Broth

1 to 2 dozen mussels
4 cups Fish Stock (page 30)
5 tablespoons butter
½ pound crevettes (or the smallest shrimp available), shelled and deveined
½ cup sliced mushrooms

¼ cup thinly sliced leeks (white part only)
3 tablespoons flour
1 cup heavy cream
1 egg yolk
1 teaspoon lemon juice
Salt and white pepper

SERVES 4 TO 6

1. Scrub the mussels with a stiff-bristled brush and remove the beards. Place them in a large pot with ½ cup of the fish stock. Bring to a boil, cover, and steam for 8 to 10 minutes, or until all the mussels have opened. Discard any that have not.

2. Remove the mussels from the pot. Strain the cooking liquid through a cheesecloth and add the liquid to the remaining stock. Shell the mussels and set them aside.

3. Melt 3 tablespoons of butter in a medium saucepan. Add the shrimp and sauté gently for 3 to 4 minutes, or until they turn pink. Remove and set aside.

4. Add the mushrooms and leeks to the saucepan, cover, and cook for 5 minutes.

5. Remove the mushrooms and leeks and set them aside with the mussels and the shrimp. Keep warm.

6. Melt the remaining 2 tablespoons of butter in the saucepan. Stir in the flour and cook for 2 to 3 minutes. Add the remaining fish stock and the cooking liquid from the mussels. Bring to a boil, stirring constantly so lumps do not form. Reduce the heat and simmer for 15 minutes.

7. While the stock is cooking, combine the heavy cream and the egg yolk. After the stock has simmered for 15 minutes, add the cream-and-egg-yolk mixture to the thickened stock, stirring vigorously. Simmer for 3 to 4 minutes more. Be careful that it does not boil.

8. Remove the mixture from the heat. Add the mussels, shrimp, mushrooms, leeks, and stir in the lemon juice. Season to taste and serve at once.

Eggs

*F*ew things can stir the blood of a French food purist more than a good argument over the correct preparations of certain dishes. Passionate debates rage in Languedoc over the number of crusts to be folded into a proper cassoulet and in Provence about the precise variety and ratio of fish and shellfish in a bouillabaisse of Marseilles. In Normandy just such passions swirl about the recipe for an omelette.

Around the turn of this century, a small inn, called the Auberge de Saint-Michel Tête d'Or, flourished at the foot of the Abbey of Mont-Saint-Michel. The proprietors were a Norman couple named Poulard, and over the years, the little inn established a reputation based upon the wife's masterful omelette-making technique. Reports filtered back to the cities of the exquisite Mère Poulard omlettes. They were so light and creamy, the reports crooned. And mysterious. How did she make them? What was her secret? Did she add extra water to the eggs? Did she whip the whites and yolks separately? Did she use a special pan? Special butter? Special salt?

When Mère Poulard died in 1931, many say that the secret died with her. The family who took over the Auberge—and now run it as Hôtel Poulard—claim she passed the secret on to them when they purchased the business. Considering the wide streak of practicality that runs through most Normans, I am inclined to believe that she would not have taken such a treasure to the grave with her—if, indeed, she ever guarded it as closely as people claim. But then there is a second restaurant at the foot of the abbey that also claims to make the true Mère Poulard omelette, so who knows?

The last time I was in Normandy, I decided to research the problem a little, so I took my family to Mont-Saint-Michel and the Hôtel Poulard for a day. I spoke to the chefs and watched them as they made the omelettes, frying them in long-handled omelette pans over an open fire in the dining room. The recipe I have included here is the result of that trip and, in my opinion, is certainly fine enough to represent the original. But, inevitably, there will be disagreement.

I have compiled a few other egg recipes, including an Omelette à l'Eau de Vive, which is prepared in the same manner as a Mère Poulard omelette but is then filled with sautéed oysters and shallots; Oeufs Pochés aux Poireaux, gently poached eggs with leeks; and a savory hard-boiled egg dish called Oeufs à la Tripe, containing onions sautéed in butter, fresh parsley, and nutmeg, but no tripe.

There is also a creamy scrambled egg dish, called Oeufs Brouillés aux Crevettes, containing shrimp, plus two classic egg preparations—Oeufs aux Miroir, in which the eggs are lightly baked until the surface takes on a mirrorlike sheen, and Les Mollets aux Herbes, served with a fragrant sauce of fresh vegetables and herbs, in which the egg whites are cooked but the yolks remain creamy.

OMELETTE DE LA MÈRE POULARD
Mère Poulard's Omelette

The preparation for this omelette is so simple it is difficult to believe it tastes so wonderful. To increase the rise of the egg mixture, do not add salt—rather, substitute lightly salted butter for sweet butter. To realize the full potential of this dish, use the freshest eggs you can find.

3 eggs, at room temperature   *2 tablespoons lightly salted*   SERVES 2
                                  butter

1. Break the eggs into a large bowl and whip until approximately 4 to 5 times their original volume. Melt the butter in a 10-inch pan or skillet, preferably of black steel, over medium-to-high heat until bubbly. Do not let the butter brown. Add the eggs, but do not stir.
2. Light the broiler. Hold the skillet approximately 1 inch above the heat source, tilting it gently from side to side and from front to back. The top surface should remain foamy, but as soon as a light brown crust begins to form along the sides of

the omelette, remove it from the heat and place under a hot broiler for 15 seconds.

3. Remove from the broiler, gently fold the omelette in half, and slide it out of the pan onto a plate. Divide in half and serve at once.

OMELETTE À L'EAU DE VIVE
Omelette with Oysters and Shallots

The basic frying method for this dish is the same as the Mère Poulard, and the addition of the oysters makes it a truly in-spired creation. *Eau de vive,* loosely translated, means oyster bed.

SERVES 2

12 medium oysters
4 tablespoons lightly salted
   butter
¼ teaspoon chopped
   shallots

1 teaspoon chopped fresh
   parsley
Fresh pepper
4 eggs

1. Shuck the oysters and reserve their juices.
2. Melt 2 tablespoons of the butter in a pan and sauté the shallots over medium heat for 1 minute. Reduce the heat and add the oysters. Cook for 3 or 4 minutes, or until they curl around the edges. Remove from the heat. Add the parsley, a few grinds of fresh pepper, and the reserved oyster juice.
3. Break the eggs into a large bowl and whip until approxi-mately 4 to 5 times their original volume. Melt the remaining butter in a 10-inch pan or skillet, preferably of black steel, over medium-to-high heat until bubbly. Add the eggs, but do not stir.
4. Light the broiler. Hold the skillet approximately 1 inch above the heat source, tilting the pan gently from side to side and front to back. While the top surface is still foamy, gently add the oyster mixture in the center.
5. As soon as a light brown crust begins to form along the sides

of the omelette, remove it from the heat and place under a hot broiler for 15 seconds.

6. Remove from the broiler, gently fold the omelette in half and slide it out of the pan onto a plate. Divide in half and serve at once.

OMELETTE FOURÉE NORMANDE
Omelette with Clams, Shrimp, Oysters, and Mushrooms

This delicious seafood omelette makes a marvelous light supper entrée. Serve with a chicory salad.

SERVES 4
(2 OMELETTES)

16 clams, as small as possible
6 tablespoons butter
½ cup mushrooms, quartered

16 small shrimps, peeled and deveined
8 oysters, shucked
8 eggs
Salt and pepper

1. Scrub the clams well. Place them in a large pot with ½ cup water. Bring to a boil and cover for 8 to 10 minutes, or until all the clams have opened. Discard those that have not. Remove the remaining clams from their shells and keep warm.

2. Melt 2 tablespoons of the butter in a pan. Add the quartered mushrooms and sauté for 4 to 5 minutes over medium heat.

3. Add the shrimp and sauté for another 4 minutes. Add the oysters and sauté for 3 minutes more. Remove the pan from the heat.

4. Break 4 eggs into a bowl and whip slightly with a fork or a whisk.

5. Melt 2 tablespoons of the butter in a pan or skillet, preferably of black steel, over a medium-to-high heat. Do not let the butter brown. Pour the eggs into the pan and whisk with a fork a few times. Allow the bottom of the omelette to cook; the top

should remain a little loose and frothy. This should take about only 4 to 5 minutes.

6. While the omelette is frying, mix the clams with the shrimp, mushrooms, and oysters. Divide the mixture and place ½ along the center of the omelette. Sprinkle with salt and pepper.

7. Fold ⅓ of the omelette over the filling, and then fold the other ⅓ over that. Slide the omelette from the pan onto a warm platter, and repeat the entire procedure for the second omelette.

OEUFS À LA TRIPE
Hard-boiled Eggs
with Onions, Parsley, and Nutmeg

The great mystery of this dish is that there is no tripe in it. It makes an excellent light lunch with a green salad and fresh bread.

SERVES 4

6 large eggs
4 tablespoons butter
½ cup finely chopped
  onions
1½ cups heavy cream

⅛ teaspoon nutmeg
Salt and pepper
1 teaspoon chopped fresh
  parsley

1. Boil the eggs for 12 minutes, cool, remove the shells, and slice into quarters. Set aside.

2. Melt 3 tablespoons of the butter in a saucepan and sauté the chopped onions for approximately 5 minutes over medium heat. Add the heavy cream, stir well, and bring to a boil. Reduce to 1 cup. Add the nutmeg and season to taste.

3. Place the eggs facedown in a buttered casserole. Pour the sauce over them and sprinkle with fresh parsley. Bake in a preheated 350°F oven for 10 minutes. Serve at once.

OEUFS AUX MIROIR
Eggs Lightly Baked in Cream

This is a very basic recipe for a classic preparation. To dress it up, you can add chopped fresh herbs, minced mushrooms, asparagus tops sautéed in butter, finely diced smoked ham, or bits of cooked fish.

½ cup heavy cream or
  Crème Fraîche (page
  23)

Salt and pepper
8 eggs

SERVES 4

1. Preheat the oven to 350°F and place 4 shirred egg dishes in to warm.
2. In a small pot bring the heavy cream or crème fraîche to a boil. Season to taste and remove from the heat.
3. Remove the dishes from the oven and divide the cream evenly among them.
4. Break 2 eggs into each dish. Place in the oven for 5 minutes. The surface of the eggs should turn cloudy but not completely opaque during this time. Remove from the oven and serve at once.

OEUFS BROUILLÉS AUX CREVETTES
Scrambled Eggs with Shrimp and Croutons

The toasted croutons add a pleasant crunch to the creamy scrambled eggs. Use the smallest shrimp you can find or simply cut larger ones into halves or thirds.

SERVES 4

4 tablespoons butter
¼ pound shrimp, shelled and deveined
½ cup croutons, made from dry French bread, diced into ¼-inch cubes

8 eggs
¼ cup heavy cream
Salt and pepper

1. Melt 1 tablespoon of the butter in a saucepan and sauté the shrimp for 2 to 3 minutes, or until they change color. Transfer to a bowl and keep warm.
2. Add the remaining butter to the pan and sauté the bread cubes until lightly browned. Remove from the heat and set aside.
3. In a water bath or double boiler over medium heat, stir the eggs constantly until they thicken evenly and their texture resembles that of cream.
4. Stir in the heavy cream and continue to stir for 1 minute more, or until the mixture is heated through. Remove from the heat and season to taste. Add the shrimp and the croutons and serve at once.

LES MOLLETS AUX HERBES
Soft-boiled Eggs
in a Fresh Herb and Vegetable Sauce

The key to this dish is yolks that remain soft, almost creamy, when served with the fragrant sauce.

4 eggs
¼ cup sorrel leaves or
    watercress with a few
    drops of lemon juice
1 sprig fresh parsley
1 sprig fresh chervil

2 leaves Boston lettuce
¼ cup spinach leaves
¾ cup Sauce à la Crème
    pour Légumes (page
    35)
Salt and pepper

SERVES 2

1. Boil the eggs for 5 minutes exactly. Remove them from the pot and place in a bowl of cold water. Reserve the hot water in the pot. When the eggs are cool, peel them.
2. Add the herbs and vegetables to the hot water and bring back to a boil. Remove from the heat and drain in a colander. Finely chop the herbs and the vegetables.
3. In a small saucepan bring the cream sauce to a boil. Reduce the heat and add the chopped herbs and the vegetables. Remove from the heat and season to taste.
4. Place the eggs in the sauce mixture over the heat for 2 or 3 minutes. Remove from the heat, place the eggs on a serving dish, and spoon the sauce over them. Serve at once.

OEUFS POCHÉS AUX POIREAUX
Poached Eggs with Leeks

SERVES 4

1 tablespoon butter
3 leeks (white part only),
　washed and very
　thinly sliced
1½ cups heavy cream

Salt and pepper
2 tablespoons white
　vinegar
8 eggs

1. Melt the butter in a saucepan. Add the sliced leeks, cover, and cook over medium heat for approximately 5 minutes, or until tender.
2. Add the heavy cream, bring to a boil, and reduce the heat. Reduce the cream to about 1 cup. Season to taste.
3. In a skillet or a shallow pot, bring 1 quart water and the white vinegar to a boil. Reduce the heat and simmer. Break each egg into a saucer. Slide the eggs, 2 at a time, into the simmering water. Poach for 3 or 4 minutes, or until done to your taste. Carefully remove the eggs with a slotted spoon and keep warm. Repeat until all the eggs have been poached.
4. Place 2 eggs on each serving plate and spoon a little leek sauce over them. Serve at once.

OEUFS EN COCOTTE ROUENNAISE
Baked Eggs, Rouen Style

This hearty egg dish can be served as an appetizer or as a light meal, particularly if you include slices of duck breast. Serve with buttered slices of toasted Pain Brié (page 273).

SERVES 2

2 tablespoons chopped bacon
2 tablespoons chopped mushrooms
2 tablespoons chopped shallots
1 tablespoon butter

1 chicken or duck liver
1 tablespoon red wine
½ cup Sauce au Vin Rouennaise (page 31)
2 eggs
2 pieces thinly sliced duck breast (optional)

1. Combine the bacon, mushrooms, and shallots and purée or chop into a fine paste.
2. Melt the butter in a medium pan and sauté the liver over medium heat for 3 minutes; it should be rare. Remove the liver, chop it very fine, and add it to the bacon-mushroom-shallot mixture.
3. Add the wine to the pan, swirl it around with a spoon over medium heat to loosen any browned bits, and add it to the liver mixture.
4. Meanwhile, heat the sauce rouennaise. Place 2 tablespoons of the warmed sauce each in the bottom of 2 8-ounce ramekins, reserving the rest. Then add ½ the liver mixture to each ramekin. Gently break 1 egg into each dish on top of the sauce and the liver mixture.
5. Place both dishes in a baking pan with about ½ inch water in it and bake in a preheated 400°F oven for 8 to 9 minutes; the yolks should remain soft.
6. If you are using them, add the duck slices to the remaining sauce to warm.
7. Remove the ramekins from the oven, place the duck breast slices around the yolks, and spoon on the remaining sauce. Serve at once.

OEUFS DURS AUX CAIEUX
Boiled Eggs in a Sauce of Mussels, Mushrooms, Shallots, Cider, and Cream

8 large eggs
24 mussels
4 tablespoons butter
1 cup thinly sliced
    mushrooms
1 teaspoon finely chopped
    shallots

4 tablespoons cider
2 tablespoons flour
1 cup milk
½ cup heavy cream
Salt and pepper

SERVES 4

1. Boil the eggs for 12 minutes, cool, remove the shells, and cut in half lengthwise.

2. While the eggs are boiling, scrub the mussels thoroughly with a stiff-bristled brush and remove the beards. Place them in a pot with ½ cup water. Bring to a boil, cover, and steam for 8 to 10 minutes, or until all the mussels have opened. Discard those that have not.

3. Shell the mussels and set aside.

4. Melt 2 tablespoons of the butter in a pan and add the sliced mushrooms. Sauté over medium heat for 4 to 5 minutes. Add the shallots and sauté for 1 to 2 minutes more. Add the cider and cook the mixture until almost dry. Remove the pan from the heat and set aside.

5. In a small saucepan, melt the remaining butter. Add the flour and stir for a few minutes over low heat. Gradually pour in the milk, stirring so it does not lump. Bring to a boil, reduce the heat, and simmer for 5 minutes. Add the heavy cream and season to taste.

6. Spread the mushroom and shallot mixture along the bottom of an ovenproof dish or casserole. Arrange the hard-boiled eggs face down on top of the mixture, and gently pour the cream sauce over the eggs.

7. Place the dish under a hot broiler for 5 minutes, or until the sauce begins to brown slightly. Serve at once.

Fish and Shellfish

*L*iving inland as we did would have left me almost entirely cut off from the rich fish and shellfish dishes of Norman cookery had it not been for the farmers' market in Saint-Hilaire-du-Harcouet. Since the market usually included at least two or three fish and seafood vendors, each with a fairly representative selection of whatever was available that day, our weekly trips became something of an incidental education for me.

The displays were always neatly arranged in wooden crates or tubs packed with crushed ice, and the vendors quickly replenished the faster-moving merchandise with supplies from behind the stalls. Such regional favorites as roussette, chien de mer, Dieppe sole, and rouget were haggled over by farmers' wives contemplating next Friday's meatless meal. Oysters, mussels, pink langoustines, and tiny gray green crevettes were scooped out of their tubs, weighed and packed into paper bags, then tucked away carefully in woven market baskets carried by black-skirted grandmothers. And presented prominently on chilled trays angled against the crates were various cuts from the larger fish—salmon, tuna, and skate. Rarely was there a mean selection.

Back home I would watch as my mother prepared the fish or shellfish I had persuaded her to buy for some recipe she had learned years ago and probably hadn't used since then. It was a fine education, but it was only after the first few months of apprenticeship near the coast that I began to realize just how extensive the subject matter really was. For each variety of shellfish there seemed to be at least half a dozen preparations, each one distinctive, each one worth knowing.

Shellfish caught in the English Channel or harvested from the numerous beds along the coast are broiled or baked on the half-shell with herb butter or a mixture of vegetables and bread crumbs, steamed open and served in cream-enriched sauces, poached with mushrooms and onions, browned in a bread-crumb-thickened sauce of rich fish broth and dry white wine, served chilled in their own shells with a sauce of fresh mayonnaise, brandy, and cream, or tossed in a salad of chopped celery and apples.

Among the fish preparations there is no lesser degree of

creativity: cod from the banks of Newfoundland are fried and topped with sautéed apples flavored with Benedictine; shad pulled from the Seine is baked and served in a sauce of sorrel and hard-boiled eggs; freshwater trout is stuffed with a mousse of sole and served with a tangy sauce of butter, cider vinegar, and herbs; pike is puréed and worked into a moist pâté that can be served hot or cold; bass is baked with shrimp butter; mackerel is poached in a rich court bouillon and served chilled; eels are sautéed with oysters and leeks; and lotte is stewed with bacon, pearl onions, cider, and crème fraîche.

Of the scores of fish and shellfish preparations that have been created, there are three in particular which stand out in any culinary context: Sole Normande—sole served with a sauce of crème fraîche garnished with a variety of regional shellfish; Moules à la Marinière—plump mussels served on the half-shell with a thickened sauce of white wine, cider vinegar, and shallots; and Marmite Dieppoise—the savory Norman seafood stew and northern counterpart of Marseillaise Bouillabaisse.

ALOSE À L'OSEILLE
Shad Fillet with a Sorrel Sauce

Shad is not as popular in Normandy as it is on the east coast of the United States, but it is served in the spring when the fish swim up the Seine to spawn. The roe are only served smoked, however, and then only as an appetizer.

4 shad fillets, approximately 8 to 10 ounces each, with the skin on
4 tablespoons butter
Salt and pepper
¼ cup cider
1 teaspoon finely chopped shallots

1 clove garlic, finely minced
2 cups sorrel, washed, ribs removed, and coarsely chopped
2 hard-boiled eggs, finely chopped
1 cup heavy cream

SERVES 4

1. Place the shad fillets skin-side up in a baking pan. Brush them with approximately 1 tablespoon melted butter and lightly season. Place in a preheated 425°F oven and bake for 5 minutes.

2. Pour the cider around the fish and continue to bake for 15 to 20 minutes more.

3. While the fish is baking, melt the remaining 3 tablespoons butter in a small saucepan. Add the chopped shallots and the garlic and cook for 1 to 2 minutes. Add the sorrel leaves, cover, and cook over a low heat for approximately 5 to 10 minutes.

4. Place the shallots, garlic, and sorrel in a food processor fitted with a metal blade and purée. Return the mixture to the small saucepan.

5. Add the chopped hard-boiled eggs and the heavy cream to the purée. Bring to a boil, reduce the heat, and simmer for 5 minutes. Season to taste.

6. Pour the sauce over the shad fillets and serve.

ANGUILLES DE LA MÈRE ANGOT
Eels Fried with Oysters and Leeks

There was a song that told of old Mère Angot selling her fish down by the docks, crying, "Sole, sole fraîche!" Whether she sold eels or not, or even whether she actually existed, is a mystery to me. I learned this recipe while I was an apprentice chef, and if it originally belonged to Mère Angot, the credit is all hers. Incidentally, the use of the fresh bread crumbs is a very old method for thickening a sauce, dating back at least to the Middle Ages.

2 dozen small to medium oysters
3 pounds eels, skinned with the heads off, washed, dried, and cut into 3-inch pieces.
Flour for dredging
6 tablespoons butter
¼ cup finely chopped leeks (green and white parts)

1 cup cider
2 teaspoons lemon juice
½ cup fresh white bread crumbs
2 tablespoons finely chopped fresh parsley
Salt and pepper

SERVES 4 TO 6

1. Shuck the oysters and reserve the oyster liquid (see page 126).
2. Dry the eel pieces and dredge them in the flour, dusting off the excess. Melt 3 tablespoons of the butter in a large skillet and add the floured eels. Sauté for 6 to 7 minutes over medium heat.
3. Add the chopped leeks and the cider and simmer for 30 minutes. Add the oysters 2 to 3 minutes *before* the eels are finished simmering. Remove the eels and oysters from the liquid with a slotted spoon and keep warm.
4. Add the liquid from the oysters, lemon juice, and bread crumbs to the skillet and mix thoroughly. Simmer over medium heat for 3 to 4 minutes. The bread crumbs will thicken the sauce.

5. Whisk in the remaining butter and chopped parsley. Season to taste. Arrange the eels and the oysters on a platter and pour the sauce over them.

NOTE   *This dish is occasionally eaten cold with potato and celery salads.*

MATELOTE D'ANGUILLES AU CIDRE
Eel Stew with Cider

Every province in France has its own particular matelote, or fish stew. However, the eels and the substitution of cider for wine give this dish an undeniably Norman flavor. Serve with boiled potatoes and a good bread to sop up the rich sauce.

SERVES 4

4 slices lean bacon
3 pounds eels, skinned with the heads off, and cut into 3-inch pieces
Flour for dredging, plus 2 tablespoons
2 tablespoons butter
¼ cup chopped onions

2 cups cider (as dry as possible)
1 teaspoon cider vinegar
2 tablespoons chopped fresh chives or scallion greens
Salt and pepper

1. In a frying pan bring the bacon and ½ cup water to a boil and simmer for 1 minute. Remove the bacon and slice into approximately ¼-inch strips. Set aside.
2. Dry the eel pieces and dredge them in flour, dusting off any excess. Melt the butter in a skillet and quickly brown the eels over medium-to-high heat.
3. Add the chopped onions and diced bacon to the skillet and cook for 3 to 4 minutes longer. Sprinkle the additional 2 table-

spoons flour into the butter, mixing well, and cook for 2 to 3 minutes.

4. Add the cider, stirring gently to avoid lumps. Bring to a boil, reduce the heat, and simmer for approximately 40 minutes.

5. Transfer the eels to a serving platter and keep warm. Add the vinegar and the chopped chives to the sauce and simmer for 3 to 4 minutes more.

6. Pour the sauce over the eels and serve.

BAR RÔTI AUX BEURRE DE CREVETTES
Roasted Bass with Shrimp Butter

Although most of the bass sold in France is caught in the Mediterranean, Norman fishing fleets take some out of the Atlantic Ocean and the English Channel. The preparation is simple, but keep an eye on the bass when it is in the oven— it will need to be basted occasionally.

1 bass fillet, approximately 1½ pounds and ½-inch thick or more
Salt and pepper
16 tablespoons butter, at room temperature
½ pound medium shrimp, shelled and deveined; keep the shells

1 teaspoon Calvados
¼ cup heavy cream
Pinch of cayenne pepper
2 tablespoons dry bread crumbs
1 teaspoons lemon juice

SERVES 4

1. Cut the bass fillet into 4 pieces. Score each fillet crosswise 3 times, with the cuts running approximately ¼ inch deep. Season with salt and pepper and arrange the fish in a lightly buttered baking dish. Set aside in a cool place.

2. Melt 2 tablespoons of the butter in a saucepan. Add the

shrimp and sauté over high heat for no more than 2 minutes. They should remain partially uncooked. Add the Calvados and cook for 1 minute more. Remove from the heat.

3. In another small saucepan bring the heavy cream to a boil. Add the shrimp shells and cook until the cream turns pinkish. Remove the saucepan from the heat and strain the cream through a fine sieve into the sautéed shrimp. Discard the shells.

4. In a blender or a food processor fitted with a metal blade, purée the shrimp mixture with the remaining butter and bread crumbs. Season to taste.

5. Spread the shrimp butter evenly over the scored surfaces of the bass fillets. Place in a preheated 400°F oven for 20 minutes. Baste occasionally with the melted shrimp butter.

6. Sprinkle with the lemon juice before serving.

PAIN DE BROCHET
Pike Loaf

This moist fish loaf can be served either hot with a cream-and-butter sauce or chilled as an appetizer or light luncheon entrée.

SERVES 6 TO 8

2 cups French bread crumbs	1½ cups heavy cream
½ cup milk	Salt and white pepper
1 pound pike	12 tablespoons butter
4 egg yolks	1½ teaspoons chopped shallots

1. Soak the bread crumbs in the milk for approximately 15 minutes.

2. Cut the pike into approximately 10 pieces, place in a food processor fitted with a metal blade, and purée. Add the egg yolks and the milk-soaked bread crumbs and continue to purée. Add ½ cup of the heavy cream, wait a few moments until it has been absorbed thoroughly, then add another ½ cup. Add 1 teaspoon salt and ¼ teaspoon white pepper. Make sure the mixture is smooth.

3. Lightly butter a 16- to 20-ounce mold of any shape and pour in the mixture. Smooth the top with a wet rubber spatula, and place the mold in a baking pan filled with water to within 1 inch of the mold's rim.

4. Bake in a preheated 350°F oven for 1 hour and 15 minutes or until a skewer or knife inserted in the center comes out clean. Remove from the oven and cool 15 minutes.

5. While the loaf is cooling, make the sauce. Bring ½ cup heavy cream and the chopped shallots to a boil and reduce the heat. Whisk the butter into the cream a small piece at a time until it has been completely incorporated. Bring the sauce back to a boil, remove from the heat, and season to taste.

6. Place an upside-down plate on top of the mold and then invert both, holding one hand under the plate. The loaf should slip out onto the plate. Serve with the cream and butter sauce.

CABILLAUD FÉCAMPOISE
Breaded Cod Fillets with Sautéed Apples and Benedictine

The city of Fécamp in Upper Normandy is not only the largest deep-sea cod port in France, it is also the home of Benedictine, the liqueur created by a Benedictine monk in the early sixteenth century. Although Benedictine is no longer distilled by the monks of the Abbey of Fécamp, the original recipe, which includes 27 herbs, such as hyssop, musk, thyme, and angelica, is still followed. In this recipe from Fécamp the Benedictine is optional; however, the fresh cod should not be replaced with salted cod.

1½ pounds cod fillets
Salt and pepper
2 eggs
1 cup fine dry bread crumbs
1 cup flour
8 tablespoons butter

1 lemon, quartered
4 cooking apples, peeled, cored, and diced into ½-inch cubes
1 tablespoon Benedictine (optional)

SERVES 4

1. Cut the cod fillets into 4 serving pieces and season lightly with salt and pepper.

2. Whisk the eggs gently in a shallow dish. Pour the bread crumbs into another shallow dish.

3. Flour the cod fillets on both sides, dusting off the excess. Dip in the eggs until completely coated, then dredge in the bread crumbs, pressing the crumbs with your hand so they adhere to the fillets.

4. Melt 4 tablespoons of the butter in a skillet and add the breaded cod. Cook over medium heat for 3 to 4 minutes on each side (longer if the fillets are particularly thick). Arrange on a platter, sprinkle with the lemon juice, and keep warm.

5. Melt the remaining butter in a skillet and add the diced apples. Sauté for 5 minutes, or until they become soft. Add the Benedictine, swirl the pan to mix the liqueur with the apples, and then spoon over the cod.

PIÈCE DE LOTTE TROUVILLAISE
Monkfish with Bacon, Pearl Onions, Cider, and Crème Fraîche

This is a hearty seafood dish, and since bacon contributes so much to the overall flavor, be sure to taste the sauce before you add salt—the bacon will have added some salt already.

SERVES 6

2 monkfish fillets, approximately 1 pound each
Flour for dredging
3 tablespoons butter
½ pound bacon, sliced into ¼-inch strips
1 dozen tiny pearl onions

½ cup cider
Fresh pepper
2 tablespoons Dijon-style mustard
1 cup Crème Fraîche (page 23)
Salt

1. Dredge the monkfish fillets in flour, dusting off the excess. Melt the butter in a large saucepan or deep skillet and brown the fish on both sides over medium heat for 10 to 15 minutes.

2. Blanch the sliced bacon in 2 cups boiling water for 3 minutes. Remove the bacon and place on paper towels to drain.

3. Place the bacon around the fillets and cook over low to medium heat for 5 minutes. Add the pearl onions and cook for 5 minutes more.

4. Pour in the cider and sprinkle the fillets with a little pepper. Cover the pan and cook for approximately 30 minutes.

5. While the fish is cooking, blend the Dijon-style mustard with the crème fraîche.

6. Remove the fillets from the pan and keep warm. Add the crème fraîche and mustard mixture, bring to a boil, and reduce by approximately ½.

7. Taste the sauce and add salt if necessary. Place the fillets back in the sauce for 3 or 4 minutes, just long enough to reheat them. Arrange on a platter and serve.

MAQUERAUX À LA DIEPPOISE
Cold Mackerel, Dieppe Style

To get the most flavor from this dish, let the fish marinate in the cooking liquid for 24 to 48 hours after cooking. If mackerel is not available, herring makes an excellent substitute. Be sure to keep the herring whole, and soak them in water for 24 hours before cooking. Serve with a cabbage or potato salad and, perhaps, a lightly spiced mustard.

SERVES 4 TO 6

8 mackerel fillets, 4 to 6 ounces each, with the skin on
½ cup cider vinegar
1½ cups dry white wine
1 cup cider
¾ cup thinly sliced onions
¾ cup carrots, peeled and sliced in ½-inch rounds

¼ teaspoon peppercorns
1 sprig fresh thyme or ¼ teaspoon dried thyme
1 bay leaf
2 cloves
1 clove garlic, crushed
¼ teaspoon coriander seeds
1 teaspoon salt
1 lemon, sliced into thin rings

1. Place the mackerel fillets in a deep baking dish and set aside.
2. In a medium pot over a high heat bring 1 cup water plus all the remaining ingredients except the lemon slices to a boil. Reduce the heat and simmer for 20 minutes.
3. While the liquid is simmering, arrange the lemon slices on the fillets. Preheat the oven to 350°F.
4. Gently pour the hot liquid, vegetables, herbs, and spices over the fillets, and place in the oven for 20 to 25 minutes.
5. Remove the fillets from the oven and let them cool in the cooking liquid at room temperature. Refrigerate overnight or, if possible, for 48 hours. During this time the fish will absorb more flavor from the liquid.
6. To serve, arrange the fillets on a serving platter, surrounded by the carrots and onions and garnished with the lemon slices. Spoon some of the cooking liquid, which will have become slightly gelatinous, on top of the fillets.

MERLAN AU PLAT
Whiting Baked with Mushrooms and Bread Crumbs

Whiting is usually cooked whole in Normandy, but since it can be a little messy to prepare it that way in the context of this recipe, I have adapted it for fillets.

SERVES 4

12 tablespoons butter
1 cup dry bread crumbs
1 teaspoon chopped fresh parsley
2 teaspoons finely chopped shallots

½ cup mushrooms, cleaned and sliced
2 pounds whiting fillets
Salt and pepper
¼ cup dry white wine

1. Melt 6 tablespoons of the butter and mix well with the bread crumbs and the chopped parsley.
2. Rub the bottom of an ovenproof dish large enough to hold

the fish fillets with approximately ½ teaspoon of the butter. Sprinkle the bottom of the dish with the chopped shallots and the sliced mushrooms.

3. Place the whiting fillets over the shallots and the mushrooms and season with a little salt and pepper. Pour in the white wine. Cover the fish with the bread crumb-and-butter mixture.

4. Dot the fillets with small bits of the remaining butter. Place in a preheated 450°F oven for 8 to 10 minutes. The bread crumbs should brown within that time. If not, place under the broiler for 2 minutes and serve.

RAIE AU BEURRE NOIR
Skate in Black Butter

Some people enjoy eating skate slightly "high," but I would recommend purchasing the freshest fish you can find. Usually, skate is sold by the wing. If it comes with the skin on, you may want to request that it be removed in the store as skate is not an easy fish to skin. If there are any leftovers, add them to a cold salad for a light lunch the next day.

¼ cup white vinegar
1 tablespoon salt
1 skate wing,
    approximately 4
    pounds, skinned
16 tablespoons lightly
    salted butter

1 teaspoon chopped fresh
    parsley
2 teaspoons capers
1 teaspoon cider vinegar

SERVES 4 TO 6

1. Bring 3 quarts water, ¼ cup white vinegar, and 1 tablespoon salt to a boil in a pot large enough to hold the skate wing. Place the skate in the water and simmer for 15 to 20 minutes.

2. Gently remove the skate from the water and drain on paper towels. At this point you may wish to remove the band of cartilage that runs through the center of wing. With a large

spatula, gently lift the top half of the wing. Remove the cartilage and replace the wing half.

3. In a skillet brown the butter over medium heat. As soon as
it begins to color, add the chopped parsley and the capers and
remove from the heat.

4. Place the skate on a serving platter and sprinkle with the
cider vinegar. Pour the browned butter over it and serve.

DARNE DE SAUMON À LA MODE D'ISIGNY
Salmon Steak, Isigny Style

This variation on a hollandaise sauce adds an elegant
touch to the poached salmon steaks.

SERVES 4

*Court Bouillon (see
    Homard Froid à la
    Chantilly, page 125)
4 salmon steaks, ½ pound
    each, cut from the
    center, if possible
1 teaspoon cider vinegar*

*1 teaspoon chopped shallots
Pinch of white pepper
3 egg yolks
16 tablespoons butter, at
    room temperature
Salt*

1. Bring the court bouillon to a boil and reduce the heat to low.
Only 1 or 2 bubbles should rise to the surface every few seconds.

2. Tie a string around each salmon steak so the steaks will be
easier to handle and will hold their shape while poaching.
Gently place the steaks in the court bouillon. Continue to
simmer for 15 to 20 minutes, making sure that the liquid covers
the fish. Do not let the liquid boil while the salmon steaks are
poaching.

3. Meanwhile, make the sauce. In a small saucepan combine
the cider vinegar, chopped shallots, and white pepper, bring
to a boil, and reduce until the liquid has nearly evaporated.

4. Scrape the reduced sauce mixture into a double boiler and add the egg yolks. With the water bath over medium heat, whisk the eggs until they thicken and take on a pale lemon color; this should take at least 2 to 3 minutes.

5. Remove from the heat and add the butter 1 tablespoon at a time, whisking vigorously until all the butter has been incorporated. Add salt to taste. Keep the sauce warm but not hot.

6. Gently remove the salmon from the court bouillon and arrange on a serving platter. Cut the string with small clean scissors and remove the skin from each steak with a fork. Spoon the sauce over the salmon and serve.

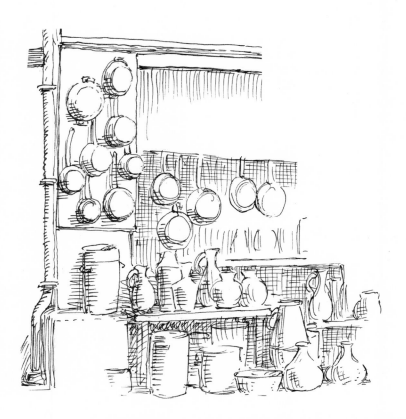

SOLE NORMANDE
Sole, Norman Style

Some controversy exists concerning the true origins of this famous Norman dish. In Normandy the mostly widely held belief is that Sole Normande is and always has been a regional preparation, but one which was at some point adapted by the haute kitchens of Paris and installed in the repertory of classical French cuisine. A conflicting theory, as propounded by Elizabeth David in her classic *French Provincial Cooking,* is that Sole Normande originated in Paris, created by Antonin Carême—not a Norman—probably during the early nineteenth century.

In either case, there are so many different recipes for Sole Normande today that a chapter could be devoted to this recipe alone. The one I have included is the recipe I learned while I was an apprentice chef. Substitute grey or Boston sole if Dover is not available.

SERVES 6

1 cup Fish Stock (page 30)
½ cup dry white wine, Muscadet or Sancerre
2 tablespoons finely chopped shallots
6 sole fillets, 8 to 10 ounces each
Salt and white pepper
1 dozen mussels, scrubbed and debearded, but still in their shells

6 whole medium to large mushrooms
6 shrimp, shelled and deveined
6 oysters, shucked
2 tablespoons Beurre Manié (page 23)
¾ cup Crème Fraîche (page 23) or heavy cream
2 egg yolks

1. In a small saucepan bring the fish stock and white wine to a boil. Reduce the heat to low and keep warm.
2. Sprinkle the chopped shallots over the bottom of a large baking dish. Roll the fillets and set in the dish, with at least ½

inch of space in between each fillet. Season lightly with salt and pepper.

3. Distribute the mussels, whole mushrooms, and shrimp around the fillets, and pour the hot fish stock and wine into the dish. Bake uncovered in a preheated 425°F oven for approximately 15 minutes. The fillets will turn white and the meat will become somewhat flaky. The mussels should open as well. Discard any that do not.

4. Remove the fillets from the baking dish and arrange on a serving platter with the mussels, mushrooms, and shrimp. Strain the liquid from the baking dish through a fine sieve into a small pot, bring to a boil, and cook over medium heat for approximately 5 minutes.

5. Add the shucked oysters while there are still 2 minutes or so to go. Then reduce the heat and whisk in the beurre manie until smooth. Simmer the sauce for 9 to 10 minutes.

6. Mix the crème fraîche with the egg yolks and pour into the sauce off the heat. Return the sauce to the stove, stirring constantly over medium heat for 4 to 5 minutes until the eggs have thickened the sauce. Do not boil. Season to taste.

7. Pour the sauce over the fillets and serve.

FILET DE SOLE AUX CREVETTES
Sole in a Crème Fraîche
and Shrimp Sauce

Since Norman sole is rarely available in this country, I would recommend grey or Boston sole instead. Flounder will do in a pinch. With regard to the shrimp, purchase the smallest you can find. This dish is more attractive with whole shrimp.

SERVES 4

4 tablespoons butter
½ pound shrimp, washed,
*   peeled, and deveined;*
*   reserve the shells*
1 teaspoon Calvados
1 cup Crème Fraîche (page
*   23) or heavy cream*
2 pounds sole fillets
Salt and pepper

2 teaspoons finely chopped
*   shallots*
½ cup Fish Stock (page 30)
*   or equal parts clam*
*   juice, dry white wine,*
*   and water*
1 tablespoon flour
1 teaspoon lemon juice

1. Melt 2 tablespoons of the butter in a saucepan and add the shrimp shells to that. Sauté for approximately 3 minutes over medium heat.

2. Add the Calvados and then the crème fraîche. Simmer for another 4 to 5 minutes, and then strain the cream through a fine sieve, pushing down on the shrimp shells with a spoon to extract more of the flavor. Discard the shells.

3. In a large baking pan arrange the sole, tucking approximately ½ inch of both ends of the fillets under. Lightly season the fillets and sprinkle the chopped shallots on top. Add the fish stock and place the pan in a preheated 350°F oven for approximately 6 to 7 minutes, or until the sole changes color.

4. Remove the pan from the oven, arrange the fillets on a serving platter, and keep warm. Drain the cooking pan, reserving the liquid.

5. Melt the remaining butter in a saucepan. Add the shrimp and sauté for 1 or 2 minutes over medium heat. Add the flour and stir well. Cook for another 2 to 3 minutes, then gradually add the reserved cooking stock and the crème fraîche, stirring gently to avoid lumps. Simmer for 5 minutes, season to taste, and add the lemon juice.

6. Arrange the fillets on a serving platter and pour the sauce over them.

FILET DE SOLES AUX OEUFS
Sole Dipped in Eggs and Flavored with a Brown Butter and Shrimp Sauce

A delicious variation on the *à la meunière* preparation. Serve with boiled potatoes or Noques (page 227).

12 tablespoons butter
6 grey or Boston sole fillets
    or flounder, 8 to 10
    ounces each
Flour for dredging
2 eggs

¼ pound shrimp, peeled
    and deveined
Juice of ½ lemon
1 teaspoon chopped fresh
    parsley
Salt and white pepper

SERVES 6

1. Melt 6 tablespoons of the butter in a skillet over a medium heat until slightly brown (nutty) in color. While the butter is melting, dredge the fillets one at a time in the flour, shaking off any excess. Whisk the eggs lightly in a shallow dish. Dip the floured fillets in the beaten eggs, allowing the excess egg to drip back into the bowl.
2. When the butter has browned, place the fillets in the skillet. The egg will begin to set immediately, so do not pack the fillets too close together.
3. Cook the sole for approximately 2 to 3 minutes on each side, or until the egg turns golden brown. Transfer the fillets to a warm platter. Continue this procedure until all the fillets have been cooked.
4. Discard the brown butter and add the remaining butter, browning as before. Add the shrimp and sauté quickly for approximately 2 to 3 minutes. Finally, add the lemon juice, chopped parsley, and season to taste. Pour the sauce over the fillets and serve.

TRUITE À LA CRÈME
Trout Cooked in Cream

Purchase the freshest trout you can for this dish, with the heads and tails left on. Serve with Champignons Rosés aux Herbes (page 214) and a Muscadet or dry Vouvray.

SERVES 4

4 whole trout, 10 to 12 ounces each, dressed and scaled
Salt and pepper
¼ cup cider
½ cup Fish Stock (page 30)

2 tablespoons Beurre Manié (page 23)
½ cup Crème Fraîche (page 23)
1 teaspoon finely chopped shallots

1. Season the cavities of the trout lightly with salt and pepper.
2. In a pot large enough to arrange the trout along the bottom side by side, bring the cider and the fish stock to a boil. Place the trout in the pot, cover, and cook over medium heat for 5 minutes.
3. Remove the trout—they will not be completely cooked—and peel off their skin. Keep warm.

4. Quickly whisk the beurre manié into the cider and fish stock and simmer for 1 minute. Add the crème fraîche and the chopped shallots. Bring to a boil, reduce the heat, and season to taste.

5. Place the trout back into the sauce and finish cooking for 8 to 9 minutes over medium heat.

6. Transfer the trout to a serving platter and pour sauce over them before serving.

TRUITE FARCIE SAINT MICHEL
Trout Stuffed with Sole

If possible, have the person from whom you buy the trout bone them from the back. I have included instructions in case the job falls to you, however.

*4 whole trout, 10 ounces
    each, dressed and
    scaled
Salt and pepper
1 sole fillet, approximately
    ¼ pound
Pinch of nutmeg
1 egg
¼ cup Crème Fraîche (page
    23) or heavy cream
6 tablespoons butter*

*1 teaspoon lemon juice or
    cider vinegar
1 tablespoon fresh chopped
    parsley
½ teaspoon fresh chopped
    chervil or ½ teaspoon
    chopped fresh
    coriander leaves
½ teaspoon tarragon or 2
    pinches dried tarragon*

SERVES 4

1. To bone the trout out from the back, hold the trout flat against the cutting board or table and insert a sharp, thin blade ¼ to ½ inch deep just in back of the head. Following the spine, draw the blade toward the tail, cutting the skin along the back. Stop just before the tail. Working the knife gently between the spine and the fillet, separate the top fillet from the bone. Turn the trout over and separate the second fillet from the bone. Place the trout on its belly and gently open the pocket. With

scissors, snip the spine in back of the head and in front of the tail. Repeat the process for all the trout. Season the pocket lightly and set aside.

2. Cut the sole fillet into 4 pieces and place in a food processor fitted with a metal blade. Add the nutmeg, egg, crème fraîche, and salt and pepper. Purée until smooth.

3. Divide the mixture evenly among the 4 trout, filling the fish from the back. Smooth the exposed stuffing with a wet spoon.

4. Place the trout in a lightly buttered baking dish in a pre-heated 325°F oven and bake uncovered for 10 minutes. Then cover with a tent of aluminum foil or buttered waxed paper and bake for another 7 to 8 minutes.

5. While the trout is baking, melt the remaining butter in a small saucepan. Add the lemon juice or cider vinegar, parsley, chervil, and tarragon and simmer for a few minutes. Remove the trout from the oven and pour the herb butter over them.

TURBOT CUIT AU BEURRE
Turbot Baked with Mushrooms

If turbot is not available, substitute halibut, fluke, or brill. This is a very simple dish to prepare and should be accompanied with boiled potatoes.

SERVES 4

1 teaspoon finely chopped shallots
4 turbot fillets, approximately ½ pound each
16 tablespoons butter, melted

Salt and pepper
4 to 6 large mushrooms, cleaned and sliced
Cider vinegar or lemon juice

1. Sprinkle the chopped shallots in an ovenproof dish large enough to hold the fillets. Place the fish on top of the shallots.

2. Pour the melted butter over the fish and season lightly. Spread the mushroom slices on top of the filets.

3. Place in a preheated 325°F oven for 30 minutes. To serve, spoon some of the butter over the fillets and sprinkle with the cider vinegar or lemon juice.

MARMITE DIEPPOISE
Fish Stew, Dieppe Style

In the early morning in Dieppe the fishermen of the old Le Pollet quarter loudly auction off their catch to buyers from the south and east. The Dieppe fleets that ply the English Channel pride themselves on bringing in higher grades of fish and shellfish—mussels, lobster, bass, whiting, turbot, mackerel, skate, and the renowned Dieppe sole—all or some of which inevitably go into the preparation of Marmite Dieppoise, a superb fish stew which rivals the bouillabaisse of Marseille.

4 tablespoons butter
2 small leeks (white part only), chopped
1 rib celery, chopped
⅓ cup chopped onion
1 tablespoon chopped shallots
2 tomatoes, peeled, seeded, and coarsely chopped
½ teaspoon curry powder
½ teaspoon chopped fresh fennel leaves or ¼ tablespoon dried fennel
1 bay leaf
4 cups Fish Stock (page 30) or equal parts clam juice, water, and white wine
1 cup hard cider or dry white wine

4 tablespoons Beurre Manié (page 23)
3 types firm white fish fillets, 1 pound each, cut into 3- to 4-ounce pieces (halibut, sole, flounder, haddock, monkfish, whiting, bass, etc.)
1 pound small shrimp, shelled and deveined
2 dozen mussels, scrubbed and debearded
1 cup Crème Fraîche (page 23) or heavy cream
1 tablespoon chopped fresh parsley
Salt and white pepper

SERVES 6

1. In a large pot melt the butter, then add the leeks, celery, onions, shallots, tomatoes, curry powder, fennel, and bay leaf. Cover and cook over low heat for approximately 15 minutes, or until the vegetables are tender.

2. While the vegetables are cooking, in a separate smaller pot combine the fish stock and cider or white wine. Bring to a boil, reduce the heat, and whisk in the beurre manié until the sauce is smooth and has thickened. Simmer for 2 to 3 minutes more. Pour the sauce into the large pot when the vegetables are tender. Bring to a boil and simmer gently for 5 minutes.

3. Add all the white fish to the stew and simmer for another 5 minutes. Add the shrimp and the mussels and continue to simmer covered for 5 minutes more.

4. Remove the pot from the heat and, with a slotted spoon, transfer all the fish and shellfish to a warm serving tureen or dish. Discard any mussels that have not opened. Keep the tureen warm. At this point the stew can be held 30 minutes before serving.

5. Stir the crème fraîche into the stewing liquid, add the chopped parsley, and season to taste. Pour the sauce into the tureen and serve at once.

COQUILLES SAINT-JACQUES À LA CRÈME
Poached Scallops in a Mushroom, Onion, and Cream Sauce

Scallops are sold in their shells in France, so you not only get the roe and the little coral tongue—which is considered to be quite a delicacy—you get the shells to serve the scallops in as well. You can serve this dish in scallop shells or a serving dish or on individual plates. If you are planning this dish as an appetizer, it will serve 4.

SERVES 2

¼ cup dry white wine
½ cup Fish Stock (page 30)
¼ cup finely chopped
  onions
1 cup mushrooms,
  quartered
1 pound sea scallops,
  quartered

2 tablespoons Beurre Manié
  (page 23)
½ cup heavy cream
Salt and white pepper

1. In a large saucepan bring the white wine, fish stock, onions, and mushrooms to a boil. Add the scallops and gently simmer for 8 to 9 minutes, or until the scallops are firm.
2. Gently pour the cooking liquid through a fine sieve into a saucepan, setting aside the scallops, mushrooms, and onions in a warm place.
3. Add the beurre manié to the liquid over medium heat, whisking quickly so lumps do not form. Add the heavy cream, season to taste, and simmer for approximately 10 minutes.
4. Pour the sauce over the scallops, mushrooms, and onions.

COQUILLES SAINT-JACQUES AU GRATIN
Gratin of Scallops

This dish improves if you allow the scallops and sauce to cool completely before browning them in the oven.

SERVES 4

½ cup dry white wine
1½ cups Fish Stock (page
  23)
2 pounds sea scallops,
  quartered
8 tablespoons butter

¼ cup chopped onions
3 tablespoons flour
1 teaspoon lemon juice
Salt and pepper
¼ cup fresh bread crumbs

1. In a large saucepan bring the wine and the fish stock to a boil. Add the scallops, reduce the heat, and simmer for 8 to 9

minutes, or until the scallops are firm. Remove the scallops with a slotted spoon and keep warm.

2. Over medium heat reduce the poaching liquid for 10 to 15 minutes, or by approximately ⅓.

3. In another pot melt 6 tablespoons of the butter, add the onions, and cook until transparent. Stir in the flour and cook for 3 to 4 minutes more.

4. Add the poaching liquid, stirring constantly so it does not lump. Bring to a boil and reduce the heat. Add the lemon juice and season to taste. Add the scallops and remove from the heat.

5. At this point, you have a choice. If you wish to serve the scallops immediately, pour them into a shallow baking dish, sprinkle with the bread crumbs, and dot with the remaining butter. Place under a hot broiler for a few minutes, or until lightly browned, and serve.

6. Or you can allow the scallops and sauce to cool completely in the refrigerator for 3 or 4 hours or, preferably, overnight; this will improve the flavor remarkably. Then place the mixture in a casserole or baking dish, sprinkle with bread crumbs, dot with butter, and bake in a preheated 425° oven for 15 to 20 minutes, or until lightly browned.

ESCARGOTS À LA CRÈME
Snails in a Cream Sauce

The snails of Normandy have been eclipsed in importance by the famous vineyard snails of Burgundy in the eyes of everyone but the Normans. Today, Norman snails are still picked off the stone walls in the towns and countryside and prepared in a crème fraîche sauce flavored with garlic and chopped herbs.

If you are preparing this dish with fresh snails, first clear the chalky substance they have sealed their shells with and then soak them in salted water for approximately 4 hours to remove the impurities. Afterward, wash them well in cold water two or three times. They are now ready for cooking. You may also use canned snails if fresh ones aren't available.

Court Bouillon

1 cup white wine
2 bay leaves
1 clove garlic, crushed
1 clove
5 stems parsley
2 stems fresh chervil or 1
    teaspoon dried chervil

2 sprigs fresh thyme or 1
    teaspoon dried thyme
1 tablespoon salt
5 peppercorns, crushed

4 dozen snails

SERVES 4

Sauce

4 tablespoons butter
1 tablespoon finely chopped
    shallots
1 tablespoon chopped fresh
    parsley
½ teaspoon fresh chopped
    chervil, or ¼ teaspoon
    dried chervil

2 cloves garlic, finely
    chopped
¼ cup hard cider or white
    wine
1 cup Crème Fraîche (page
    23)
Salt and pepper

1. In a large saucepan bring 4 cups water and all the court bouillon ingredients to a boil. Reduce the heat and simmer for 30 minutes.

2. Add the snails and simmer for approximately 2 hours and 30 minutes, or until tender.

3. When the snails are tender, remove the court bouillon from the heat. If fresh snails are used, pull the snails from their shells with a long needle. Trim approximately ¼ inch off their tails —this is called the cloaca—and return the snails to the bouillon to cool.

4. If you want to save the snail shells, wash them well in cold water and then boil in water for another 15 minutes.

5. Remove snails from the bouillon and drain well.

6. To make the sauce, melt the butter in a skillet. Add the drained snails and toss quickly in the butter for about 15 seconds.

7. Add the shallots, parsley, chervil, and garlic and sauté for 2 to 3 minutes.

8. Add the cider or white wine and simmer for about 5 minutes more.

9. Add the crème fraîche, return to a boil, and reduce the liquid by approximately ½. This should take 10 to 15 minutes over medium heat.

10. Remove from the heat and season to taste. Serve with fresh bread for dipping.

HOMARD À LA CRÈME
Lobster Simmered in Cream

In Normandy this dish is prepared with small lobsters the fishermen call *demoiselles de Cherbourg*—"young ladies of Cherbourg." The lobstermen take most of these out of the coastal waters extending from the city of Dieppe in Upper Normandy to the Cotentin peninsula, of which Cherbourg is the largest city and port. Other than their size, however, these lobsters possess no special qualities, so any fresh 1- to 1¼-pound lobster will be fine.

SERVES 4

*4 fresh lobsters, 1 to 1¼
    pounds each
2 tablespoons butter
4 large mushrooms, finely
    chopped*

*1 teaspoon Calvados
2 tablespoons cider
1½ cups heavy cream
Salt
Pinch of cayenne pepper*

1. Wash the lobsters well under cold running water. Cook in a large pot of boiling water for 3 to 4 minutes. Remove and let cool. With a large, sharp knife cut them in half lengthwise. Remove the gelatinous sac near the head and discard. Remove the greenish brown tomalley and reserve; if there are black eggs, or roe, save them as well. Crack the claws, remove the meat from the claws and tail, and cut all the lobster meat into bite-sized pieces.
2. In a large skillet melt the butter over low heat and add the lobster meat. Cover and cook over low heat for 15 minutes. Transfer the lobster to a platter and keep warm.
3. While the lobster is cooking, bring ½ cup water to a boil and add the finely chopped mushrooms. Bring the water back to a boil and cook for 3 minutes more. Strain the liquid through a sieve and reserve. Discard the mushrooms.
4. Chop the lobster tomalley and the roe, if any, and place them in the skillet in which you cooked the lobster meat. Add the reserved mushroom liquid, the Calvados, and the cider and boil for 4 to 5 minutes. Add the heavy cream and simmer for 5 minutes more over medium heat.

5. Add the lobster meat to the sauce, simmer for 5 minutes over low to medium heat, then season to taste with salt and cayenne pepper.

HOMARD FROID À LA CHANTILLY
Chilled Lobster in a Cream and Mayonnaise Sauce

A splendid warm-weather entrée or appetizer. Refill the empty lobster shells with the chilled meat and Calvados-laced sauce for a memorable presentation.

Court Bouillon   SERVES 4
1 tablespoon salt
1 sprig fresh thyme or ½ teaspoon dried thyme
5 peppercorns
1 bay leaf
1 small onion, peeled and sliced

2 ribs celery, sliced
1 small carrot, peeled and sliced
2 tablespoons cider vinegar
5 stems parsley

4 lobsters, 1 pound each

Sauce Chantilly
1 egg yolk, at room temperature
1 teaspoon cider vinegar
¼ teaspoon salt
Dash white pepper

½ cup peanut oil
½ teaspoon Calvados
½ cup heavy cream, whipped

1. In a large pot add all the court bouillon ingredients to 12 cups water and bring to a boil. Simmer for 20 minutes. Add the lobsters and simmer for 20 minutes more. Remove the lobsters and cool.

2. When the lobsters have cooled, cut them in half lengthwise with a large sharp knife. Remove the gelatinous sac near the head and discard. Remove the greenish brown tomalley and reserve; if there are black eggs, or roe, save them as well. Crack the claws, remove the meat. Keep the meat from each lobster half separate. Cut all the lobster meat into bite-sized pieces. Keep cool.

3. To make the sauce Chantilly, combine the egg yolk with the cider vinegar, salt, and white pepper in a bowl. Slowly drizzle in the peanut oil, whisking vigorously as you pour it; the mixture should thicken into a mayonnaise.

4. When all the oil has been incorporated, add the Calvados and gently fold in the whipped cream. The sauce should be light and fluffy. Chop the lobster tomalley and fold it into the sauce.

5. Place the lobster meat back into the hollow shells. If there is any roe, put that back in also. Spoon the Sauce Chantilly over the meat. Place the lobsters in the refrigerator to chill for 30 minutes before serving.

Oysters on the Half-Shell

The inhabitants of Normandy have been eating and enjoying oysters ever since the Celts began to harvest them from their fertile beds along the coast centuries ago. Every year from autumn until spring, the oysters are gathered and then prepared according to the countless recipes that have evolved throughout the province. Oysters are included in sauces and soups, as entrées and garnishes for other seafood dishes, on skewers, in quiches, and even in fritters. But in the bistros and cafés of the ports and coastal towns, the style is to eat the oysters on the half-shell—raw with a squeeze of lemon or a cider vinaigrette, or broiled and garnished with herbs, chopped vegetables, or cream—followed by a good bottle of corked cider or dry white wine.

The following four recipes are all based on these simple half-shell preparations and can be served as either appetizers or light entrées, a dozen oysters constituting an entrée. Explained below are the few preliminary steps common to all these recipes:

Before opening an oyster, scrub the outside of the shell with a stiff-bristled brush to remove any dirt or loose bits of shell. If both halves of the shell move apart easily, discard the oyster. To open the shell, insert a small, sharp knife at the pointed end of the oyster and cut through the muscle holding the two shell halves together, being careful not to stab the oyster itself. Gently remove the flat top shell and discard it; try to spill as little of the oyster liquid as possible. At this point the oysters are now ready to be served raw on the half-shell.

If you plan to bake the oysters in their shells, remove them from the shells and place them in a bowl with the strained liquid from the shells. Boil the shells in salted water for about 10 minutes and rinse under cold running water. You are now ready to proceed with the recipe itself.

VINAIGRETTE À HUÎTRES
Vinaigrette for Oysters on the Half-Shell

Just sprinkle a little vinaigrette on a raw oyster the way you would lemon juice.

1 cup cider vinegar
1 tablespoon finely chopped shallots

1 teaspoon crushed peppercorns

Mix all the ingredients together and then leave at room temperature for 3 days.

Enough vinaigrette for 2 to 3 dozen oysters.   YIELD

HUÎTRES À L'OSEILLE
Poached Oysters on the Half-Shell with Sorrel

SERVES 3

3 dozen small to medium oysters
2 tablespoons butter
1 teaspoon finely chopped shallots
2 cups sorrel, washed, ribs removed, and coarsely chopped

1 cup Fish Velouté (page 34)
½ cup Crème Fraîche (page 23) or heavy cream
¼ cup dry bread crumbs
Salt and pepper

1. Shuck and clean oysters and their shells, reserving the liquid.
2. Melt the butter in a saucepan and add the shallots, sautéeing them over medium heat for 1 or 2 minutes.
3. Add the oysters and sauté for 2 minutes. Remove from the heat and replace the oysters in their shells along with a little of the sautéed shallots.
4. In a large saucepan bring the reserved oyster liquid to a boil, add the sorrel, and cover. Cook for 5 minutes. Strain and allow the sorrel to cool. Finely chop the sorrel by hand or place in a food processor fitted with a metal blade; do not purée.
5. Bring the fish velouté to a boil in a saucepan and add the chopped sorrel. Simmer over medium heat for 5 minutes. Gradually add the crème fraîche or the heavy cream and simmer for 3 to 4 minutes more. Taste the mixture and season.
6. Place 1 to 2 tablespoons of the sauce in each shell and then sprinkle with the dry bread crumbs.
7. Place in a preheated 450°F oven until lightly browned, 5 to 10 minutes. Serve at once.

HUÎTRES AU BEURRE D'ÉCHALOTES
Oysters on the Half-Shell with Shallot Butter

2 dozen small to medium
    oysters
Sprigs fresh tarragon or
    pinch of dried
    tarragon per oyster
12 tablespoons butter, at
    room temperature

2 tablespoons finely
    chopped shallots
2 tablespoons finely
    chopped scallions
    (white and green parts)
1 teaspoon lemon juice
Salt and pepper

SERVES 2

1. Shuck and clean the oysters and their shells, reserving the liquid.
2. Place 2 sprigs fresh tarragon or a pinch of dried tarragon on each shell and put the oyster on top. Pour a little of the liquid into the shell and repeat the procedure for all the oysters.
3. Cream the butter in a bowl, add the chopped shallots, scallions, and lemon juice, and mix well. Season to taste.
4. Distribute the butter mixture evenly over the oysters, 1 to 1½ teaspoons for each oyster.
5. Place the oysters on a sheet pan in a preheated 450°F oven for 7 to 8 minutes. Serve at once with French bread to soak up the liquid.

GRATIN D'HUÎTRES CHAUDIVERT
Oysters on the Half-Shell with Spinach, Cider, and Crème Fraîche

SERVES 2

2 dozen small to medium
   oysters
2 cups fresh spinach leaves
Salt
2 tablespoons butter
1 tablespoon finely chopped
   shallots

¼ cup fresh bread crumbs
½ cup cider or white wine
1 cup Crème Fraîche (page
   23)
Freshly ground pepper

1. Shuck and clean the oysters and their shells, reserving the liquid.
2. Wash the spinach well, removing the stem from each leaf. In a large pot bring 2 cups salted water to a boil and add the spinach. Wait for the water to boil again, then drain at once. Let the spinach leaves cool and chop fine.
3. Melt the butter in a large skillet and add the finely chopped shallots. Sauté for 1 minute over medium heat.
4. Add the oysters with 2 tablespoons of the bread crumbs and sauté for 2 minutes more. Remove from the heat and place the oysters back in their shells with a little of the bread crumb-and-shallot mixture.
5. In a small saucepan bring the reserved oyster liquid and cider or white wine to a boil. Continue to boil until the liquid is reduced to approximately ¼ cup.
6. Add the crème fraîche, bring to a boil, and reduce to approximately ½ cup.
7. Add the chopped spinach to the crème fraîche mixture and cook for another 1 to 2 minutes. Remove from the heat and fill the oyster shells with the mixture.
8. Sprinkle the tops of the oysters with the remaining bread crumbs, then bake in a preheated 450°F oven until lightly browned, 5 to 10 minutes.
9. Before serving, grind a little fresh pepper on top of each oyster.

PIED DE CHEVAL
SAINTE-ADDRESSE
Horses' Hooves, Sainte-Addresse Style

The "horses' hooves" in the title are actually large, flat, very plump oysters, cultivated along the coasts of Normandy and Brittany. In the coastal towns they are commonly breaded and then sautéed in butter. Cider vinegar is sprinkled on them at the table from a cruet, and as is the case here, they are dipped in freshly whipped cream. When you shop, pick out the largest oysters you can find.

4 dozen very large oysters
Salt and pepper
3 eggs
2 tablespoons flour
*2 cups fine dry bread
    crumbs*

8 tablespoons butter
½ cup heavy cream
1 tablespoon cider vinegar

SERVES 4

1. Shuck the oysters and discard the liquid. Dry the oysters on paper towels and season with salt and pepper.
2. In a medium bowl mix the eggs and the flour with a whisk. Put the bread crumbs into another bowl.
3. Coat each oyster with the egg mixture and then dredge in the bread crumbs. After each oyster is dipped, place it on waxed paper. Repeat the process until all the oysters have been breaded.
4. In a large heavy skillet melt 4 tablespoons of the butter over medium heat. Add half the oysters and brown on both sides. Then set them aside to drain on paper towels.
5. Wipe the loose bread crumbs out of the skillet with a cloth or paper towels. Then melt the remaining butter and brown the rest of the oysters.
6. While the oysters are browning, whip the cream to a stiff peak. Do not add sugar.
7. Just before serving, sprinkle a few drops of the cider vinegar on each oyster.
8. Serve the oysters with whipped cream for dipping.

SALADE DE QUEUES DE LANGOUSTINES
Apple and Langoustine Salad

Langoustines from the English Channel are quite similar to prawns in appearance and taste. Only about 4 inches long when mature, they are usually boiled and then served chilled in Normandy, with a mayonnaise-based sauce for dipping. Fresh langoustines may be available in this country, but in most cases they will be frozen. Large shrimp are an excellent substitute in this dish, however, as are crayfish. Either of these fresh would be superior to frozen langoustines.

SERVES 4

6 cups Court Bouillon (½ recipe Homard Froid à la Chantilly, page 125)
3 pounds langoustines or 2 pounds medium shrimp
1 egg yolk, at room temperature
2 tablespoons cider vinegar
Salt and pepper

½ cup peanut oil
¼ cup celery, washed and diced
2 apples (Granny Smith or Golden Delicious), peeled, cored, and diced
¼ teaspoon prepared horseradish

1. In a large pot bring the court bouillon to a boil. Add the langoustines or the shrimp and let the court bouillon return to a boil. Reduce the heat and simmer for 5 minutes.
2. Remove the langoustines or shrimp, cool, then shell and devein. Chop the meat into ½-inch pieces and keep chilled.
3. In a large bowl combine the egg yolk, cider vinegar, ¼ teaspoon salt, and ⅛ teaspoon pepper. Mix well with a whisk.
4. Gradually add the peanut oil, whisking until creamy.
5. Combine the diced celery, apples, and the langoustines or shrimp. Pour the dressing over them and add the prepared horseradish. Mix well with a spoon or fork and taste for seasoning. Serve at room temperature.

LANGOUSTINES GRILLÉES AU BEURRE
Langoustines Broiled with Herb Butter and Bread Crumbs

Don't remove the shells of langoustine—or large shrimp or prawns. They are served with them on to retain more of the herb butter and enhance the flavor.

3 pounds langoustines, large shrimp, or prawns
16 tablespoons butter
Salt and pepper
1 tablespoon finely chopped shallots
1 clove garlic, finely chopped

Pinch of nutmeg
2 tablespoons chopped fresh parsley
1 teaspoon chopped fresh chervil or ¼ teaspoon dried chervil
¼ teaspoon chopped chives
¼ cup fresh bread crumbs

SERVES 4 TO 6

1. Wash the shellfish and cut them in half lengthwise, but do not remove the shells. Devein and arrange on an ovenproof platter or baking dish with the meat facing up.
2. Cream the butter in a bowl and season with a little salt and pepper. Add all the remaining ingredients except the bread crumbs and mix well.
3. With a small knife spread the butter evenly over the shellfish. Sprinkle the bread crumbs on top.
4. Place under the broiler but not too close to the heat source. Broil for 8 to 10 minutes. Serve at once.

GRATIN DE LANGOUSTINES
Langoustine Gratin
with a Calvados- and Sherry-laced Cream Sauce

If possible purchase the shellfish—langoustines, prawns, or shrimp—with the heads still attached. They enrich the sauce.

SERVES 4

Salt
2 bay leaves
3 pounds langoustines,
  shrimp, or prawns
6 tablespoons butter
2 tablespoons finely
  chopped carrots
1 teaspoon finely chopped
  shallots
½ teaspoon fresh tarragon
  or ¼ teaspoon dried
  tarragon

1 tablespoon tomato paste
1 teaspoon Calvados
2 tablespoons dry sherry
2 cups Fish Stock (page 30)
  or equal parts clam
  juice, dry white wine,
  and water
Pinch of cayenne pepper
2 tablespoons flour
¾ cup Crème Fraîche (page
  23) or heavy cream

1. In a large pot bring 2 quarts water, 2 teaspoons salt, and 2 bay leaves to a boil. Add the shellfish and simmer for 5 minutes. Drain the shellfish and cool.
2. When the shellfish have cooled sufficiently, remove the heads and shells and reserve. Refrigerate the meat until you are ready to use it.
3. Melt 4 tablespoons of the butter in a large saucepan and add the shells and the heads. Sauté for 2 minutes. Add the carrots, shallots, and tarragon and cook for 3 to 4 minutes more.
4. Add the tomato paste, Calvados, and dry sherry. Stir well and simmer for 3 to 4 minutes more. Pour in the fish stock and add a small pinch of cayenne pepper. Bring to a boil, reduce the heat, and simmer for 30 minutes.
5. Remove the liquid from the heat and strain through a cheesecloth into a bowl, pressing down on the shells and heads with a spoon to extract as much flavor as possible.
6. Melt the remaining butter in a medium saucepan and stir in the flour. Blend well and cook over medium heat for 3 to 4

minutes. Pour in the sauce and whisk vigorously to avoid lumps. Bring to a boil, reduce the heat, and simmer for 5 minutes. Add half the crème fraîche. Simmer for 2 to 3 minutes, then season to taste with salt.

7. Spoon the sauce into individual serving dishes, reserving approximately ½ cup, and keep warm.

8. Add the remaining crème fraîche to the remaining sauce and simmer for 1 or 2 minutes. Add the shellfish to the sauce to reheat.

9. Pour the sauce and shellfish mixture into a shallow casserole or ovenproof dish. Place under the broiler until lightly browned. Serve immediately with the individual dishes of sauce.

MOULES FARCIES GRANVILLAISE
Mussels Baked with Herb
and Garlic Butter

As an appetizer, this dish will serve 6; as an entree, 2 to 3.

2 quarts (4 pounds) mussels
¾ pound (3 sticks) butter
½ cup chopped fresh parsley
2 tablespoons chopped fresh chervil
¼ teaspoon chopped fresh thyme
4 cloves garlic, finely chopped
1 teaspoon salt

1. Scrub the mussels in cold water with a stiff-bristled brush and remove beards. In a large pot with ½ cup water bring the mussels to a boil. Cover and steam for 8 or 9 minutes. Stir once with a long spoon. Remove the mussels with a slotted spoon and discard any that have not opened. Remove the top shell from each mussel and discard. Strain the cooking liquid through a fine sieve and reserve. Keep the mussels cool in the refrigerator.

2. In a medium bowl whisk together the butter, parsley, chervil, thyme, garlic, reserved mussel liquid, and salt.

3. Place approximately 1 teaspoon of the herb butter over each mussel. Bake in an ovenproof dish in a preheated 450°F oven for 5 minutes. Serve with fresh French bread to soak up the butter.

MOULES À LA MARINIÈRE
Mussels, Fisherman-Style

This classic recipe of Normandy is simply conceived and based on the superb mussels raised in the beds around Isigny, Villerville, Dives, and elsewhere along the Norman coast.

SERVES 2 TO 3

2 quarts (4 pounds) mussels
2 tablespoons chopped
    shallots
1 bay leaf
1 cup dry white wine
Freshly ground pepper
2 tablespoons chopped
    parsley

⅛ teaspoon cider vinegar
2 tablespoons Beurre Manié
    (page 23)
4 tablespoons butter
Salt

1. Scrub the mussels in cold water with a stiff-bristled brush and remove beards. In a large pot bring the mussels, chopped shallots, bay leaf, white wine, a few grinds of pepper, and parsley to a boil. Cover and steam for 8 to 9 minutes. Remove the mussels with a slotted spoon and discard any that have not opened. Remove the top shell from each mussel and discard. Keep the mussels warm on a platter.
2. Add the cider vinegar to the cooking liquid and bring back to a boil. Reduce the heat and whisk in the beurre manié. Once the liquid has thickened, add the butter, remove from the heat, and season with salt. Spoon the sauce over the mussels and serve at once.

MOULES POULETTE
Mussels in a Cream and Egg Sauce

This is a variation of the marinière preparation but much richer. It is often eaten as a soup and served with a good French bread for dipping.

2 quarts (4 pounds) mussels
¼ cup dry white wine
2 tablespoons chopped
    onions
2 egg yolks
Pinch of pepper

½ cup heavy cream
¼ teaspoon lemon juice
1 tablespoon fresh chopped
    parsley
Salt

SERVES 4

1. Scrub the mussels in cold water with a stiff-bristled brush and remove beards. In a large pot bring ½ cup water, the white wine, and the onions to a boil. Add the mussels, cover, and steam for approximately 5 minutes. Remove the mussels with a slotted spoon, and discard any that have not opened. Shell the others and keep warm.
2. Reduce the cooking liquid over high heat for 3 to 4 minutes. Strain through a fine sieve and pour into a smaller pot.
3. Combine the egg yolks, pepper, heavy cream, lemon juice, and chopped parsley. Pour the mixture into the reduced cooking liquid over low heat, stirring constantly for 3 minutes, or until it thickens. Add salt to taste.
4. Divide the mussels among 4 serving bowls. Pour the hot sauce over them and serve at once.

LE FEUILLETÉ NORMAND
Mussels and Scallops in a Cream Sauce Served in a Puff Pastry Shell

This dish requires little preparation but yields elegant results. Serve as an appetizer or entrée.

SERVES 4

10 to 12 ounces Puff Pastry Dough (page 24, approximately ¼ recipe; or purchase frozen) or 4 frozen patty shells
1 egg yolk
1 dozen mussels
2 tablespoons finely chopped onions
4 peppercorns, crushed
¼ cup dry white wine
1 teaspoon finely chopped shallots

8 shrimp, shelled and deveined
¼ cup mushrooms
¼ pound sea scallops
2 tablespoons Beurre Manié (page 23)
½ cup heavy cream
¼ teaspoon lemon juice
Salt and white pepper

1. On a floured board or table, roll out the puff pastry dough ⅛ to ¼ inch thick. With a small knife cut out 4 3- by 4-inch rectangles. Brush with a mixture of egg yolk and ¼ teaspoon water, and bake in a preheated 450°F oven for 8 to 10 minutes, or until the rectangles are golden brown. Cut them in half and set aside, keeping the top and bottom of each together. Keep warm.

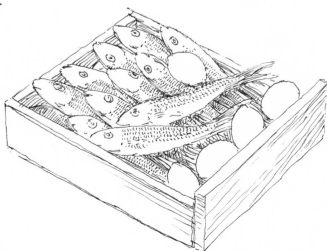

2. Scrub the mussels well in cold water with a stiff-bristled brush and remove the beards. Place them in a heavy pot with ¼ cup water, the chopped onions, and the crushed pepper-corns. Cover and steam for 5 minutes, or until the mussels open. Discard any that do not and reserve the liquid.

3. Remove the mussels from their shells and set aside. Strain the liquid through cheesecloth and pour it back into the pot.

4. Add the white wine, shallots, shrimp, mushrooms, and scal-lops. Poach until the fish is firm; this should take approximately 5 minutes.

5. Remove the shrimp, scallops, and mushrooms from the poaching liquid and set aside with the mussels.

6. Bring the liquid to a boil, reduce the heat, and whisk in the beurre manié until thickened and smooth. Simmer for 2 to 3 minutes. Stir in the heavy cream and the lemon juice, season to taste, and return the shellfish and mushrooms to the sauce.

7. Spoon the shellfish and the sauce over the bottom half of the puff pastry rectangles. Replace the top half of the rectangle and serve.

Poultry
and
Game Birds

*H*ad Normandy contributed nothing else to the French table but the Rouennais duckling, serious eaters would undoubtedly still accord the province a grateful nod. Highly prized throughout France and Europe for its tender and flavorful flesh, the Rouennais, like its Breton counterpart, the Nantais duckling, is actually a cross between wild and domestic varieties. Many Norman farmers keep small flocks, but most are raised outside the city of Yvetot in Upper Normandy not far from Duclair, another town famous for breeding its own variety of Rouennais duckling. Similar in flavor and texture, both the Rouennais and the Duclair birds are well suited to roasting at a high temperature for a short time. In the finer restaurants of the province, thin slices of blood-rare breast meat are served with deep, rich sauces prepared from the blood and enhanced with dry red wines or reduced stock. In many cases, the duck liver is finely minced and stirred into the sauce at the last moment, as in the classic Caneton Rouennais à l'Ancienne. Less frequently these ducklings are braised, usually in a dry cider, stock, or water, with seasonal vegetables and herbs. A particularly rustic recipe included here, and one which my mother favors, calls for the duckling to be roasted —on a rotisserie over a hearth, if possible—and served with a tangy sauce of apple jelly, stock, and pan juices.

Normandy can also be credited with an excellent breed of chicken from the Auge Valley. Raised on farms in most areas of the province today, the Auge Valley chicken is even popular with townspeople, who will keep two or three in their small backyards for fresh eggs. But egg-laying is only a temporary reprieve, for these older hens are usually destined for some as yet unplanned Sunday dinner, probably in a poule au pot flavored with turnips, carrots, leeks, and potatoes. Younger birds, although occasionally stewed, are usually sautéed, roasted, or fricasseed and accompanied by a wide variety of sauces made from crème fraîche, cider vinegar, stocks, cider, and herbs. Stuffings can run the gamut from the sturdy medieval Farc Normand, made from bread, liver, and roasted onions, to a delicate shrimp and cream mousse.

Gray Norman geese, raised around the city of Alençon, also play an important part in Norman cookery. Younger geese

are often roasted and basted with butter and their own rendered fat, while the older farmyard birds are prepared in much
the same manner as fowl—slowly stewed or braised in cider,
broth, or water.

Despite the efforts of generations of avid Norman sports-
men, the woods still teem with pheasant, quail, and red-legged
partridge. There are numerous recipes for game birds in the
province, but the majority of the preparations I have seen call
for a foil of rich sauces heightened with heavy cream, Calvados, or wine.

CANETON ROUENNAIS
À L'ANCIENNE
Roast Duckling Served Pink,
with Cider and Apples

The traditional recipe for this dish requires that the duckling
be smothered rather than decapitated, a method that allows
the flesh to retain as much of the blood as possible. By sending
the duckling off in this manner, the already fine flavor of the
flesh is enhanced, and the color remains quite red, even after
cooking.

However, since Rouennais ducks are not widely available
in this country, and since it is highly unlikely that many people
would go rushing out to smother them even if they were, I
recommend that you purchase the best duck you can from a
butcher or grocery store. I have prepared this dish with a
white Pekin duck, and the results were quite satisfactory.

Comparing this recipe with the following preparation
from Duclair, you will notice a marked difference in cooking
times. This is due to the addition of a stuffing here, as well the
need to render more fat from the white Pekin duck. Yet even
with the increased cooking time, this recipe should yield meat
that is fairly rare. If you prefer your duck a little more well-
done, simply add 10 to 15 minutes to the cooking time.

Stuffing

½ pound bacon, cut
    crosswise in small
    strips
1 cup chopped onions

2 cups diced French bread
Pinch of nutmeg
Salt and pepper

Duckling

5 -pound White Pekin
    duckling

1 tablespoon hard cider or
    Calvados

Sauce

1 tablespoon finely chopped
    shallots
2 cups hard cider
1½ cups Brown Stock (page
    27)

½ finely chopped duck
    liver
2 tablespoons butter

1. To make the stuffing, sauté the bacon in a skillet over low heat until the fat has been rendered. Discard ½ the fat and add the chopped onions. Sauté until light brown.

2. In a large bowl mix the onions, bacon, and fat from the pan with the diced bread. Add the nutmeg, mix well, and season to taste.

3. Wash the duckling and dry the cavity with a paper towel. Cut away as much fat from the opening as possible. Prick the skin with a fork or small knife to render as much fat as possible while cooking. Season the cavity with salt and pepper and sprinkle with cider or Calvados. Pat the stuffing into the cavity. Sew or fasten the opening with skewers.

4. Place the duckling in a shallow roasting pan and bake in a preheated 450°F oven for approximately 1 hour and 15 minutes. Drain off some of the rendered fat as the duck roasts. Remove the duckling and keep warm.

5. To make the sauce, drain all but 2 tablespoons of the fat from the baking dish and place the dish over medium heat. Add the chopped shallots and sauté for approximately 5 minutes, or until they brown.

6. Add the cider, bring to a boil, and simmer for approximately 10 minutes, or until reduced by ½. Stir in the brown

stock and continue to simmer for another 10 minutes.

7. While the sauce is simmering, remove the stuffing from the duck and place it in the center of a warm platter. Cut the duckling into serving pieces and arrange them around the stuffing. Keep warm.

8. When the sauce has finished simmering, strain it through cheesecloth back into a small saucepan and remove as much fat from the surface as possible. Add the minced liver and the butter to the sauce, return to a medium heat, and whisk gently. Do not boil. The sauce should remain on the heat for about 1 minute, just long enough to poach the liver. Remove from the heat and season to taste. Pour the sauce over the duckling and serve at once.

CANARD À LA DUCLAIR
Duck, Duclair Style

Ducklings from the town of Duclair located in the lower Seine valley are almost as celebrated as their Rouennais counterparts. In fact, this dish is a simpler, more rustic version of Caneton Rouennais à l'Ancienne and was originally prepared on a rotisserie in a hearth.

SERVES 2

4- to 5-pound Moscovy or
    Mallard duckling
Salt and pepper
6 tablespoons butter, at
    room temperature
1 duck liver, finely chopped
1 tablespoon finely chopped
    shallots
Pinch of nutmeg
¾ cup Brown Stock (page
    27)
1 teaspoon lemon juice

1. Wash and dry the duckling. Season the duck cavity with salt and pepper and rub 2 tablespoons of the butter on the skin.

2. Place the duckling on its side in a small roasting pan in a preheated 450°F oven for 10 minutes. Then turn it over on the other side and roast for 10 minutes longer. Turn the duck over so the back is facing up and roast for 10 minutes more, and

finally roast breast up for 10 minutes. Remove the duck from the oven and let it cool on a rack with a plate underneath to catch the juices as they drain. Set aside the pan with the cooking juices in it.

3. At this point the duckling will be roasted medium-rare. If you prefer the meat more well-done, place the sliced meat under the broiler just before serving.

4. Meanwhile, finely chop the duck liver with a knife; do not purée in a food processor. Combine it with the chopped shallots, 2 tablespoons of the butter, and the nutmeg. Set aside.

5. With a sharp knife slice each duck breast into 6 or 7 thin strips. Remove the legs from the carcass and cut them at the joint into 2 pieces each. Set aside and keep warm. Cut the carcass into smaller pieces and set aside also.

6. Drain as much fat from the roasting pan as possible. Place the smaller pieces of the duck carcass in the pan with any of the juices that have drained out of the duck while it was cooling. Place the pan over medium heat and add the brown stock and the lemon juice. Cook for 10 minutes and remove the pieces of duck with a slotted spoon. Add the liver and shallots and return the pan to the heat for 1 minute, stirring well. Stir in the remaining 2 tablespoons of butter and season to taste.

7. If the duck is too rare, put it under the broiler. If not, arrange on a platter, pour the sauce over it, and serve.

CANARD À LA JELÉE DE POMMES
Roast Duck with Apple Jelly Sauce

Serve this savory dish with Apple Fritters (page 259) and Braised Turnips (page 220).

SERVES 4

4- to 5-pound white Pekin duckling
Salt and pepper
1 cup Apple Jelly (page 272)
1 clove

1 teaspoon cider vinegar
1 cup Brown Stock (page 27)
1 teaspoon Calvados

1. Wash and dry the duckling, and season the cavity with salt and pepper. Truss the duckling and place in a roasting pan in a preheated 375°F oven for approximately 1 hour and 45 minutes, or until the juices run clear. Baste every 15 to 20 minutes.

2. Remove the duckling from the oven and allow it to cool on a rack for 15 minutes before carving. Pour off as much of the fat as possible from the roasting pan and set the pan aside.

3. In a small saucepan, melt the apple jelly and add the clove and the cider vinegar. Simmer for 5 minutes.

4. Place the roasting pan on the stove and add the brown stock, scraping up the browned bits with the back of a wooden spoon. Bring the liquid to a boil and reduce by approximately ⅓.

5. Add the reduced brown stock and cooking juices and the Calvados to the apply jelly. Bring to a boil and stir well. Simmer for 5 minutes, then season to taste. Remove from the heat.

6. To serve, cut the duckling into serving portions, arrange on a platter, and pour the sauce over.

POULE AU BLANC
Fowl Simmered with Vegetables and Served with a Cream Sauce

A famous peasant dish prepared throughout France. However, the addition of the cream sauce is strictly Norman. A fowl makes a tastier broth, but if none is available, use a chicken.

SERVES 4

4- to 5-pound fowl
4 turnips, trimmed and peeled
4 small leeks, approximately 5 inches long after trimming, tied together
6 small carrots, trimmed and peeled
1 parsnip, trimmed and peeled
8 small potatoes, peeled
Bouquet garni (1 sprig fresh thyme, 5 to 6 stems parsley, 1 bay leaf tied between 2 or 3 green leek leaves)

1 small onion, peeled, halved, and studded with 1 clove in each half
5 tablespoons flour
1 cup Crème Fraîche (page 23)
Salt and pepper

1. Place the fowl in a large pot and cover with water. Bring to a boil, reduce the heat, and simmer for 1 hour and 30 minutes. Skim the top occasionally.
2. Add the turnips, leeks, carrots, parsnip, potatoes, bouquet garni, and the onion. Simmer for approximately 1 hour more.
3. Skim approximately ¼ cup melted chicken fat from the surface of the broth, and in a separate pot combine it with the flour. Stir over medium heat for 2 or 3 minutes and set aside.
4. Approximately 10 minutes before the chicken is done, remove 3 cups cooking broth and gradually stir it into the flour and fat mixture over medium heat. Bring to a boil, reduce the heat, and simmer for 5 minutes. Stir in the crème fraîche and simmer for another 5 minutes. Season to taste.

5. Remove the fowl and the vegetables from the broth. Cut the fowl into serving pieces and all the vegetables with the exception of the potatoes into bite-sized pieces. Arrange on a platter and serve with the sauce. Reserve the leftover broth for a future meal.

POULET À LA FICELLE
Chicken with a Creamy Mustard and Cider Vinegar Sauce

In the traditional recipe for this dish, the chicken is tied with a length of string and then lowered into the broth to cook; hence the *ficelle,* or string, in the title. I revised this recipe somewhat, however. Now the chicken is merely simmered, and very little of the rich chicken broth is served with the meat. As a result, this dish should provide you with 1 or 2 quarts of excellent stock. Serve the chicken hot or cold.

4-pound chicken
4 small leeks,
    approximately 5 inches
    long after trimming,
    tied together
2 cups turnips, peeled and
    diced into ½-inch
    cubes
2 cups carrots, peeled and
    cut into ½-inch
    cylinders

1 pound small new
    potatoes, peeled
2 bay leaves
1 clove
¼ cup cider vinegar
1 teaspoon Dijon-style
    mustard
Pinch of nutmeg
Salt and pepper
1 cup heavy cream

SERVES 4

1. Place the chicken in a large pot and add 12 cups water. Bring the water to a boil, reduce the heat, and simmer for 30 minutes. Skim the surface occasionally.

2. Add the leeks, turnips, carrots, potatoes, bay leaves, and clove to the pot and simmer for 1 hour more.

3. In a bowl whisk together the cider vinegar, mustard, nutmeg, and salt and pepper. Gradually add to that approximately ¼ cup of the chicken broth and the heavy cream, continuing to whisk as you do. Set aside.

4. Remove the chicken and the vegetables from the broth. Cut the chicken into serving pieces and arrange on a platter with the vegetables. Serve with the sauce.

FRICASSÉE DE POULET À COTENTIN
Chicken Simmered in Cider with Shallots and Mushrooms

A simple, rustic dish from the Cotentin peninsula. If possible, purchase fresh chanterelles rather than ordinary mushrooms. They will add quite a bit of flavor to the dish.

SERVES 2

2 ½-pound chicken, quartered
Salt and pepper
3 tablespoons flour
2 tablespoons Graisse Normande (page 21) or butter
½ cup cider or dry white wine

1 cup Chicken Stock (page 29)
6 shallots, peeled
1 clove
1 cup whole small mushrooms or chanterelles cut into 6 or 8 pieces
¼ cup heavy cream

1. Season the chicken quarters with salt and pepper. Place the flour in a shallow dish and coat the chicken completely, shaking off any excess and reserving it.

2. Melt the graisse normande or butter in a large skillet and brown the chicken. Add the reserved flour to the fat, stir, and cook for 3 minutes.

3. Pour the cider or wine and the chicken stock over the chicken and stir until the sauce begins to thicken. Add the shallots and the clove and simmer over low-to-medium heat for 20 minutes.

4. Add the mushrooms or chanterelles and simmer for 25 minutes more.

5. Remove the chicken from the pan and keep warm. Discard the clove. Add the heavy cream, simmer for another 5 minutes, and season to taste. To serve, arrange the chicken on a platter and pour the sauce over it.

ÉTOUFFÉE DE VOLAILLES AUX HERBES
Chicken Simmered in an Herb Sauce

2 ½-pound chicken,
    quartered
Salt and pepper
2 tablespoons flour
2 tablespoons butter
1 tablespoon chopped
    shallots
1 small clove garlic,
    chopped
½ teaspoon cider vinegar
½ cup cider
½ cup Brown Stock (page
    27)

2 teaspoons chopped fresh
    parsley
½ teaspoon chopped fresh
    chervil or ¼ teaspoon
    dried chervil
¼ teaspoon chopped fresh
    tarragon or ⅛ teaspoon
    dried tarragon
2 teaspoons chopped fresh
    chives

SERVES 2

1. Season the chicken with salt and pepper. Place the flour in a shallow dish and coat the chicken completely, shaking off any excess and reserving it.

2. Melt the butter in large skillet and brown the chicken. Add the shallots and garlic, stir, and cook for 2 to 3 minutes.

3. Add the reserved flour, stir, and cook for another 3 minutes.

4. Add the cider vinegar, cider, and brown stock. Bring to a boil and stir the sauce until it thickens. Reduce the heat, add the parsley, chervil, tarragon, and chives, and simmer covered for 45 minutes.

5. Remove the chicken and arrange it on a serving platter. Season the sauce to taste, then pour it over the chicken and serve.

SUPRÊMES DE VOLAILLES AUX CREVETTES
Breast of Chicken with Shrimp and Leeks

I first prepared this dish when I was an apprentice and have seen numerous variations ever since. In my opinion, though, the sweet poached leeks in the sauce make this recipe very special.

SERVES 4

¼ pound shrimp, peeled and deveined (for the stuffing), plus 4 whole shrimp, peeled and deveined (for the garnish)
¾ cup heavy cream
Salt and pepper
4 chicken breasts, approximately ½ pound each, boned with skin on

1 cup Chicken Stock (page 29)
2 tablespoons leeks, (green part only), cut into ⅛-inch slices
1 tablespoon Beurre Manié (page 23)

1. In a food processor fitted with a metal blade, purée ¼ pound shrimp with ¼ cup of the heavy cream and salt and pepper until smooth.

2. Loosen the skin on the chicken breast, but do not remove. Divide the purée among the breasts, spreading each with a thin layer between the loosened skin and the meat. Refrigerate the breasts for at least 1 hour.

3. In a good-sized shallow saucepan bring the stock and the leeks to a boil, and reduce the heat to low. Place the chicken breasts in the stock, skin-side up. Make sure the breasts are sitting well up out of the liquid so the shrimp mixture does not run off into the sauce. Cover and poach gently for 20 to 25 minutes.

4. Remove the breasts, place on a platter, and keep warm. Add the 4 whole shrimp to the stock and poach for 3 to 4 minutes. Remove them from the stock and butterfly with a small knife. Place 1 shrimp on top of each chicken breast.

5. Stir the beurre manié into the stock, whisking well so it does not lump. Add the remaining cream and simmer for 4 to 5 minutes. Season to taste and pour the sauce over the chicken breasts before serving.

SUPRÊMES DE VOLAILLES CAMEMBERT
Breast of Chicken Stuffed with Camembert

A tangy dish from the Auge Valley, where the best Camembert cheese is made. Serve it with a sparkling Vouvray or a light Bourgueil from the Loire Valley, if available.

SERVES 4

4 chicken breasts, approximately ½ pound each, skinned and boned
Salt and pepper
¼ pound Camembert cheese, with rind removed and cut into 4 ⅛-inch pieces

Flour for dredging
2 eggs, beaten
1 cup fresh bread crumbs
8 tablespoons butter

1. With a large, flat knife, butterfly each chicken breast: Hold the breast flat against a cutting board with one hand, and beginning at the thick edge of the breast, slice through to within approximately ½ inch of the opposite side. Open as you would a book.
2. Place each breast between sheets of waxed paper or plastic wrap and flatten slightly with a meat mallet or the flat edge of a heavy knife. Season with salt and pepper.
3. Place 1 piece of Camembert on ½ of the breast, and fold the other ½ over it. Dredge the breast completely in the flour, shaking off the excess. Repeat the process for all the breasts.
4. Dip each floured breast into the beaten egg, then completely cover with the bread crumbs.
5. Melt the butter in a heavy skillet over medium heat. When the butter begins to brown, add the chicken breasts, cooking for approximately 10 minutes on each side. Remove to a serving platter. If you choose, you can pour the brown butter over the breasts.

LE FARC NORMAND
Roast Chicken
with Onion and Chive Stuffing

This is a recipe that dates from the late Middle Ages and is still very popular in Normandy today. The roasted onions in the farc—or stuffing—are traditionally cooked in the hearth by burying them under hot ashes overnight.

2 medium onions
6 tablespoons butter, at
*   room temperature*
1 teaspoon chopped chives
1 chicken liver, finely
*   chopped*
1 egg, beaten
3 cups fresh French bread,
*   or a good white bread,*
*   diced into ¼-inch*
*   cubes*

1½ cups Chicken Stock
*   (page 29)*
Salt and pepper
4- to 5-pound chicken

SERVES 4 TO 6

1. Roast the whole onions in their skins in a preheated 350°F oven for 1 hour and 30 minutes, or until tender. When the onions have cooled, remove the skin and coarsely chop the flesh.
2. In a bowl mix the chopped onions with 4 tablespoons of the butter. Add the chopped liver, beaten egg, bread cubes, ½ cup of the stock, and salt and pepper. Mix well.
3. Season the cavity of the chicken with salt and pepper and place the stuffing inside. Do not pack it in too tightly. Sew or fasten the opening with skewers and truss the chicken.
4. Rub the remaining butter on the chicken and season the outside with salt. Place it in a roasting pan in a preheated 350°F oven for 45 minutes, basting often.
5. Pour the remaining stock into the pan and continue to baste every 15 minutes for 45 minutes.
6. Remove the stuffing and serve with the chicken and seasoned pan juices.

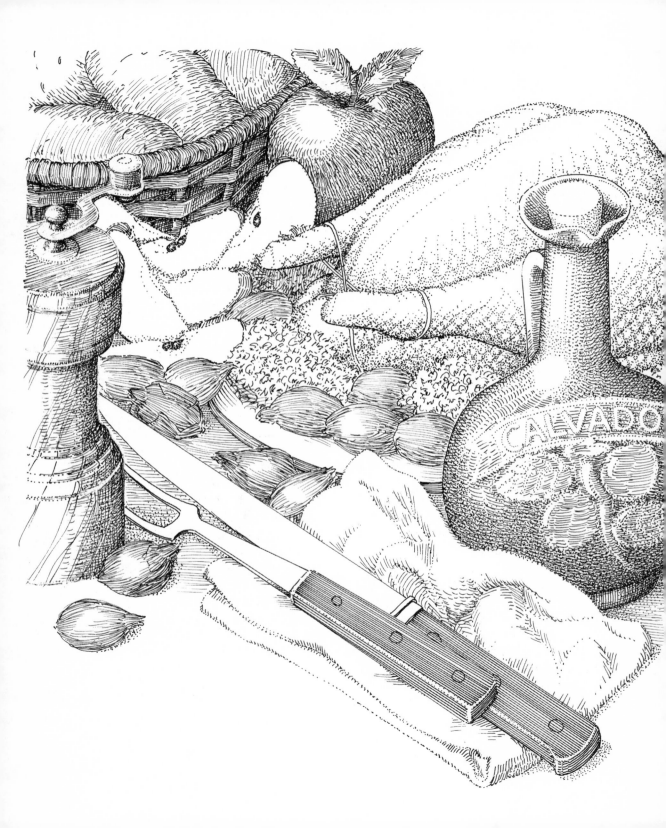

POULET RÔTI AUX OIGNONS
Roast Chicken with Onions

This is another recipe from the Auge Valley, where the finest chickens in Normandy are still bred. To vary this dish, add new potatoes while the chicken is cooking or cored and quartered apples 15 minutes before it is removed from the oven.

4- to 5-pound chicken
Salt and pepper
1 chicken liver (optional)
1 teaspoon Calvados
4 tablespoons butter
4 medium onions, peeled
    and quartered, or 24
    pearl onions, peeled

1 teaspoon confectioners'
   sugar
1 cup heavy cream

SERVES 4

1. Trim the fat from around the cavity of the chicken and season inside with salt and pepper. Place the liver in the cavity and sprinkle the inside with the Calvados. Sew or fasten the opening with skewers, and truss the chicken.
2. Coat the chicken with 2 tablespoons of the butter and place it in a roasting pan. Arrange the onions around the chicken and dot with the remaining butter. Place in a preheated 400°F oven and cook for 25 to 30 minutes.
3. Lightly dust the chicken with the confectioners' sugar—if you have an empty salt or pepper shaker, use that to sprinkle the sugar. Place the chicken back in the oven. At the end of 30 minutes, baste the chicken with the pan juices. Return it to the oven for 30 minutes more and continue basting several times while it is cooking. During that time, the onions should turn golden brown.
4. Remove the chicken from the oven and cut into serving pieces. Place the onions around the chicken with the liver. Keep warm.
5. Add the heavy cream to the pan and bring to a boil on the stove. Scrape the bottom of the pan with a wooden spoon to loosen the browned bits. Season to taste and serve the sauce with the chicken and onions.

OIE À LA MODE D'ALENÇON
Braised Goose, Alençon Style

A Christmas favorite. For a variation on the stuffing, substitute chestnuts for the apples. You will need a large roasting pan with high sides for this recipe.

SERVES 6 TO 8

6- to 7-pound goose
2 medium onions, chopped
1 pound ground pork
1 cup milk
4 cups dry bread, diced
2 eggs, beaten
2 leaves sage or ¼ teaspoon
    dried sage
¼ teaspoon Pâté Spice (see
    Pâté de Campagne,
    page 41)
1 goose liver, finely
    chopped (optional)

6 apples (Granny Smith,
    Golden Delicious, or
    McIntosh); 1 apple
    should be peeled,
    cored, and diced into
    ¼-inch cubes, the
    other 5 should be cored
    and quartered
Salt and pepper
4 cups dry cider
4 cups Brown Stock (page
    27)
5 tablespoons flour

1. Cut approximately ¼ cup goose fat from around the cavity and melt it slowly in a heavy pot. Add the chopped onions and sauté until lightly browned.

2. Add the ground pork, stir, and brown over medium heat. Set aside.

3. In a medium saucepan bring the milk to a boil, pour it over the dry bread, and mix well. Add the beaten eggs, sage, pâté spice, chopped goose liver, and diced apple. Combine the mixture with the ground pork and onions and season to taste.

4. Stuff the goose, but do not pack the stuffing too tightly. Sew the opening with string.

5. Place the goose under the broiler in a pan for approximately 15 minutes, or until it begins to brown. (If your broiler cannot accommodate the goose, place it in a preheated 450°F oven for approximately 30 minutes.)

6. While the goose is browning, bring the cider and brown stock to a boil in a pan large enough to hold the goose. Add the goose, cover—if you don't have a cover, you can use aluminum

foil—and braise in a preheated 325°F oven for approximately 15 minutes a pound. Baste it occasionally with the cooking liquid.

7. While the goose is braising, skim about ¼ cup melted goose fat from the surface of the cooking liquid and pour it into a small saucepan. Add the flour to the fat and stir over medium heat for 4 to 5 minutes, or until it turns pale brown. Set aside.

8. In another pan cook the 5 quartered apples in ½ cup water for 15 to 20 minutes. Run the mixture through a food mill or purée in a food processor fitted with a metal blade. Keep warm.

9. When the goose is done, remove it from the braising liquid and strain the liquid. Try to remove as much fat as possible from the surface. Pour the liquid over the flour-and-fat mixture and bring to a boil, stirring to avoid lumps. Simmer for 5 to 10 minutes and season to taste.

10. While the sauce is simmering, remove the stuffing and cut the goose into serving pieces. Serve with the sauce and the puréed apples.

FAISIN À LA MODE DES BÉNÉDICTINS
Pheasant with Shallots, Mushrooms, Garlic, Cream, and Benedictine

Roast pheasant has an extremely deep, rich flavor, and the accompanying sauce complements it beautifully. The combination of caramelized sugar and cider vinegar was often used to make a kind of sweet-and-sour sauce during the Middle Ages, but the addition of the crème fraîche and the Benedictine dates this sauce somewhat later than that. Serve with a dry white wine or fruity red wine.

SERVES 4

2 pheasants 2½ pounds each
Salt and pepper
Flour for dredging
4 tablespoons butter
4 whole shallots, peeled
2 cloves garlic, peeled
2 cups whole small mushrooms, cleaned and trimmed at the stem

1 cup cider
1 cup Brown Stock (page 27)
2 tablespoons sugar
1 tablespoon cider vinegar
2 tablespoons Benedictine
¼ cup heavy cream

1. Cut each pheasant into 4 pieces by first slicing it in half lengthwise down the backbone, then cutting each breast in half. Season lightly with salt and pepper and then dredge in flour, shaking off any excess.
2. Melt the butter in a skillet that can be put in the oven. Brown the the pheasant sections on all sides over medium heat. Add the whole shallots and garlic and sauté for 1 or 2 minutes. Place the skillet in a preheated 450°F oven for 20 to 25 minutes. Remove the pheasant and keep warm on a platter. Set aside the skillet with the cooking juices, garlic, and shallots.
3. In a small saucepan bring the mushrooms to a boil in ½ cup water. Boil hard for 5 minutes, then drain the water into the skillet in which the pheasant was cooked. Transfer the mush-

rooms to a dish and place the skillet back on the heat.

4. Add the cider and brown stock to the skillet, stir, bring to a boil, and simmer for approximately 20 minutes. The liquid will reduce by ⅓ to ½.

5. Meanwhile, cook the sugar and 1 tablespoon water in a small saucepan until the sugar begins to turn a nutty color. Slowly stir in the cider vinegar and remove the pot from the heat.

6. Remove the shallots and garlic from the skillet and discard. Add the liquid in the skillet to the sugar-and-vinegar mixture. Place it back on the stove and add the Benedictine, mushrooms, and heavy cream. Simmer for 10 minutes more and season to taste. To serve, pour the hot sauce over the pheasant.

FAISAN RÔTI CALVADOS
Roast Pheasant Flavored with Calvados

Pheasant can dry out very quickly when roasted, so you must keep an eye on it. The cooking time I have suggested yields a somewhat rare bird. So if you prefer your meat more well-done, add 9 to 10 minutes to the roasting time—but be careful.

2½-pound pheasant
Salt and pepper
4 tablespoons butter
*2 teaspoons chopped
    shallots*
*2 tablespoons finely
    chopped mushrooms*

1 teaspoon Calvados
Pinch of nutmeg
*1 cup Crème Fraîche (page
    23)*

SERVES 2

1. Season the cavity of the pheasant lightly with salt and pepper. Truss the pheasant with a string the same way you would a chicken so it does not lose its shape while roasting. Rub the skin all over with 1 to 2 tablespoons butter.

2. Place the pheasant in a roasting pan in a preheated 450°F oven for 10 minutes per pound. Turn the bird on one side to

start, then change sides midway through the roasting process. It will brown more evenly this way.

3. When the pheasant has cooked, remove it from the pan and let it cool for a few minutes. Then with a sharp knife carefully remove both legs and the breast meat. Keep the meat warm. Use scissors to cut up the carcass in smaller pieces.

4. Place the roasting pan on the stove over medium heat and add the carcass. Cook the pieces in the pan drippings for 3 to 4 minutes.

5. Add the chopped shallots, mushrooms, and Calvados. Stir and cook for 4 to 5 minutes.

6. Add the nutmeg and the crème fraîche, bring to a boil. Boil for 2 minutes. Strain the sauce through a cheesecloth into a bowl, then whisk in the remaining butter. Season to taste.

7. Slice the breasts into thin strips and arrange on a platter with the legs. Pour the hot sauce over the meat and serve.

PERDREAUX COTENTIN
Partridge, Cotentin Style

Partridge is one of the more common game birds in the woods of Lower Normandy, and my brother Daniel, who fancied himself the hunter of the family, would bring a few home and ask my mother to prepare them. This is one recipe I recall her making.

In France game birds are, under most circumstances, cooked rare, the same as ducklings. If you prefer more well-cooked meat, add 10 to 15 minutes to the cooking time.

4 young partridges, ¾
    pound each
Salt and pepper
2 apples (Granny Smith,
    Golden Delicious, or
    McIntosh) peeled,
    cored, and halved
6 tablespoons butter

1 tablespoon sugar
1 teaspoon cider vinegar
1½ cups Brown Stock (page
    27)
1 teaspoon Calvados
¼ cup Crème Fraîche (page
    23) or heavy cream

SERVES 4

1. Season the cavities of the partridges with salt and pepper. Place half an apple in each cavity and truss the birds with string the same way you would a chicken.

2. In a heavy pot melt 4 tablespoons of the butter. Add the partridges and lightly brown over low heat for 10 to 15 minutes.

3. Cover and continue to cook over low heat for 30 minutes (longer if you prefer your meat well-done).

4. Remove the partridges and let them cool on a platter that will catch the juices as they drain.

5. Meanwhile, in a small saucepan cook the sugar with 1 teaspoon water until it begins to turn a nutty color. Stir carefully so it does not splash. Slowly add the cider vinegar and stir.

6. Add 1 cup brown stock to the sugar mixture, bring to a boil, and simmer for 10 to 15 minutes, or until reduced by approximately ⅓.

7. While the stock is simmering, remove the legs and breast meat from each partridge with a sharp knife. Arrange on a platter with the cooked apple halves. Cut up the carcasses into small pieces with a knife or scissors, and return them to the pot in which the partridges were cooked. Add the juices that drained from the partridges while they were cooling.

8. To the partridge cooking pot add the remaining brown stock, Calvados, and crème fraîche and bring to a boil. Reduce the heat and simmer for 5 minutes. Pour the liquid through a strainer into the caramelized sugar and stock mixture, and simmer for 4 or 5 minutes more. Season to taste. To serve, pour the sauce over the partridge meat.

Meat
and
Game

*Q*uality meats are so plentiful in Normandy today that it is difficult to imagine a time when Normans had to be content with less. Shops prominently display well-trimmed cuts of Norman beef and veal, their fine flavor and texture most often compared to that of the famed Charolais of Burgundy. Farmers proudly parade their fat sheep, lambs, and pigs past buyers from other provinces at early-morning livestock markets, and housewives from the towns and countryside alike routinely prepare savory dishes of venison and rabbit—game that is readily available in most markets or from local farmers.

Rich preparations have come to underscore this abundance. Across Norman tables pass such widely varying dishes as roasts of beef and venison basted with crème fraîche, chunks of veal or lamb stewed in dry cider and heavy cream, pork braised with prunes and fresh vegetables, pot roasts marinated for days in court bouillons of cider vinegar, stocks, and herbs, and tender pink hams cured in sea salt for weeks and then simmered in cider.

Throughout the province's long history, however the Norman people have known leaner times, and out of these times has emerged a tradition of preparing such meats as tongue, feet, tripes, brains, liver, and sweetbreads. While this aspect of Norman cookery was sparked principally by the poorer farmers' need to use as much of the animals slaughtered in the fall as possible, there was also the even more immediate need of survival. One story tells of how the ninth-century inhabitants of Caen, following what must have been a particularly fierce encounter with a marauding band of Vikings, were left with no food to sustain them. Even after a thorough search of the area, the survivors were able to find only a few cows' stomachs and feet, several pig skins and some vegetables—items the Vikings had either overlooked or simply tossed away. Out of desperation the townspeople decided to combine everything in one pot, and then share it among themselves. They survived, the story goes, and that desperate meal has since evolved into a dish many Normans feel is worthy of its own recipe competition every year in the city those Vikings almost destroyed— Tripes à la Mode de Caen.

This tradition has yielded other artful preparations as well, including calf's brains sautéed in brown butter; poached beef tongue served with a piquant sauce of capers, cornichons, cider vinegar, and chives; sweetbreads wrapped in cabbage leaves and braised in cider and stock; and the famous Tête de Veau Normande—actually three separate preparations of calf's head.

BLANQUETTE DE VEAU AUX NAVETS
Veal Simmered with Turnips and Mushrooms

A rich, creamy stew traditionally served with boiled potatoes on the side. You can add other vegetables to this dish also, such as carrots, pearl onions, or salsify.

2 ½ pounds veal chuck or shoulder, cut into 1-inch cubes
1 pound medium turnips, peeled and cut into 4 or 5 pieces each
Bouquet garni (1 sprig fresh thyme, 5 to 6 stems parsley, and 1 bay leaf tied between 2 or 3 green leek leaves)

¾ pound mushrooms, cleaned and quartered
2 tablespoons butter
2 tablespoons flour
1 cup Crème Fraîche (page 23) or heavy cream
Salt and pepper

SERVES 4

1. In a large pot bring the cubed veal and 2 cups water to a boil. Skim the impurities from the surface, reduce the heat to medium.
2. Add the turnips and the bouquet garni and simmer gently for approximately 1 hour. Add a little water if too much evaporates.

3. Add the mushrooms and simmer for 10 to 15 minutes more.

4. Transfer the meat, turnips, and mushrooms to a bowl and keep warm. Discard the bouquet garni.

5. Skim as much fat as possible from the surface of the broth. Set aside.

6. In a saucepan melt the butter. Stir in the flour and cook for 2 to 3 minutes over medium heat. Gradually, pour in the broth, stirring quickly so lumps do not form in the sauce. Bring to a boil, reduce the heat, and simmer for 10 to 15 minutes.

7. Add the crème fraîche and simmer for 10 minutes more. Add the meat, turnips, and mushrooms to the sauce and season to taste.

VEAU AUX SALSIFIS
Veal Stew with Salsify

Salsify, or oyster plant, is an extremely popular vegetable in Normandy, particularly during late summer, when the new crop is available in the shops. If you cannot find fresh salsify, canned will work quite well in this dish.

SERVES 4 TO 6

Flour for dredging
3 pounds veal shoulder, cut
*　　into 1-inch cubes*
4 tablespoons butter
½ cup chopped onions
1 clove garlic, chopped
1 cup cider
2 cups Brown Stock (page
*　　27) or water*
Bouquet garni (1 sprig
*　　fresh thyme, 5 to 6*
*　　stems parsley, and 1*
*　　bay leaf tied between 2*
*　　or 3 green leek leaves)*

2 tablespoons tomato purée
1 pound salsify
1 teaspoon lemon juice
Salt and pepper
2 teaspoons chopped fresh
*　　parsley*

1. Lightly flour the veal.
2. Melt 2 tablespoons of the butter in a skillet and quickly brown the veal on all sides. Transfer the veal to a heavy pot.
3. Melt the remaining butter in the skillet and add the onions and the garlic. Sauté for approximately 5 minutes over medium heat. Add the cider to the onions and loosen the browned bits in the bottom of pan with a wooden spoon. Pour the cider mixture over the veal and add the brown stock or water, bouquet garni, and tomato purée. Bring to a boil and stir. Reduce the heat and simmer for 15 minutes.
4. Meanwhile, peel the salsify (if you have gloves, wear them; salsify will stain your hands) and cut it into ½-inch pieces. In a large pot bring 8 cups salted water containing the lemon juice to a boil and add the salsify. After 4 or 5 minutes, drain and add the salsify to the stew.
5. Cover the stew and continue to simmer for 45 minutes, or until the meat and salsify are tender. Season to taste and sprinkle with the chopped fresh parsley.

QUASI DE VEAU AUX CAROTTES
Braised Veal with Carrots

This rustic braised veal dish from Lower Normandy is flavored with tender young carrots and lettuce and served with new potatoes.

8 tablespoons butter
3-pound veal shoulder, tied
5 cups small carrots, peeled and cut into ¼-inch slices
12 new potatoes, peeled and halved
1 cup Boston lettuce, shredded

¼ cup cider
½ cup Brown Stock (page 27) or water
1 teaspoon Calvados (optional)
Salt and pepper

SERVES 4 TO 6

1. Melt 4 tablespoons of the butter in a heavy pot. Add the veal and brown on all sides.
2. Arrange the vegetables around the veal, and add the cider, brown stock, and Calvados. Bring to a boil, reduce the heat, cover, and simmer for 1½ to 2 hours.
3. Remove the meat. Stir in the remaining butter and season to taste. Slice the veal and serve with the vegetables and the braising liquid.

CÔTE DE VEAU VALLÉE D'AUGE
Veal Chop, Auge Valley Style

A fresh-tasting simple dish from the Auge Valley, this preparation combines some of the tastiest elements of that region. And it can be ready to serve in under an hour.

SERVES 4

4 veal chops, approximately
½ pound each.
Salt and pepper
Flour for dredging
4 tablespoons butter
16 small pearl onions,
peeled
24 whole small mushrooms,
cleaned and trimmed

½ cup celery root, cut into
¼-inch cubes, or ½
cup celery, cut into
¼-inch slices
1½ cups heavy cream
½ cup peas, fresh if
possible

1. Season the veal chops with salt and pepper. Dredge them in the flour, shaking off any excess.
2. In a large casserole or pot, melt the butter and brown the veal chops on both sides.
3. Add the pearl onions, mushrooms, and celery root. Cover and cook over medium heat for 10 minutes.
4. Pour in the heavy cream and cook for another 15 minutes.
5. Add the fresh peas and continue to cook for 10 minutes more.
6. Remove the veal chops and season the sauce to taste.

CÔTE DE VEAU AU POIRÉ
Veal Chop with Mushrooms, Pears, and Pear Brandy

This dish is a variation on the Côte de Veau Vallée d'Auge from around the town of Domfront, where farmers raise pears for poiré, the light Norman pear brandy.

4 veal chops, approximately ½ pound each
Salt and pepper
Flour for dredging
2 tablespoons Graisse Normande (page 21) or butter
1 cup mushrooms, cleaned and thinly sliced
¼ cup cider

½ cup Brown Stock (page 27)
1 tablespoon finely chopped shallots
1 pear, peeled, halved, cored, and cut into ¼-inch slices
1 tablespoon poiré or pear brandy

SERVES 4

1. Season the veal chops with salt and pepper. Dredge them in the flour, shaking off any excess.
2. In a large casserole or pot, melt the graisse normande or butter. Add the chops and brown on both sides over medium heat. Reduce the heat, cover, and let the chops cook for 2 to 3 minutes.
3. Add the sliced mushrooms. Cover and cook for 5 minutes more.
4. Stir in the cider and the brown stock and cook uncovered for 3 or 4 minutes. Add the shallots and arrange the pear slices on top of the chops. Continue to cook uncovered for another 10 minutes.
5. Add the poiré or pear brandy and cook for 5 minutes more. Remove the chops, season the sauce to taste, and serve.

JARRET DE VEAU
À LA CIBOULETTE
Veal Shank with Chives and
a Warm Vinaigrette Sauce

After the veal shank has cooked completely, remove as much of the tender marrow as possible with a knife or a small spoon. It makes a wonderful garnish for the sauce. This dish is usually served with slices of beets which are cooked separately.

SERVES 4

2 ½–3 pounds veal shank
4 medium carrots, peeled
4 leeks, approximately 5 inches long (white and green parts), washed, trimmed, and tied together
16 small new potatoes, peeled

2 onions, peeled, halved, and studded with 1 clove in each half
Bouquet garni (1 sprig fresh thyme, 5 to 6 stems parsley, and 1 bay leaf tied between 2 or 3 green leek leaves)

Sauce
¼ cup cider vinegar
¼ teaspoon crushed black peppercorns
½ cup peanut oil

3 tablespoons chopped chives
Salt

1. Wash the veal shank well in cold water.
2. In a heavy pot bring the shank and 10 cups water to a boil. Reduce the heat and simmer for 30 minutes. Skim the impurities from the surface occasionally.
3. Add the carrots, leeks, potatoes, onions, and bouquet garni. Continue to simmer for 45 to 60 minutes, or until the shank is tender.
4. After the shank has cooked completely, remove from the pot and extract as much of the marrow as possible. Chop the marrow into small pieces and set aside. Remove the onions from the liquid and discard the cloves. Finely chop the onions to be used in the sauce and reserve. Discard the bouquet garni.

5. To make the sauce, in a small bowl combine the cider vinegar, pepper, ¼ cup cooking liquid, and chopped onions. Gradually add the oil, whisking vigorously to achieve a creamy
texture. Add the marrow and the chives and season to taste.
Serve with the shank and the vegetables.

This dish can also be served cold.   N O T E

ROUELLE DE VEAU DUCEYENNE
Veal Shank, Ducey Style

Fresh tarragon makes a world of difference in this recipe, but
if that is not available, the next best thing is to use the leaves
found in bottles of tarragon vinegar. Barring that, resort to
dried tarragon.

*4 veal shanks,
    approximately 10
    ounces each
Salt and pepper
Flour for dredging
2 tablespoons Graisse
    Normande (page 21) or
    butter
¼ cup chopped onions
¼ cup chopped leeks
    (white and green parts)*

*1 tablespoon chopped
    tarragon
1 cup cider
2 cups Brown Stock (page
    27)
Bouquet garni (1 sprig
    fresh thyme, 5 to 6
    stems parsley, and 1
    bay leaf tied between 2
    or 3 green leek leaves)*

S E R V E S   4

1. Sprinkle the bone marrow of each shank with salt; this will
prevent the marrow from melting. Dredge each shank in the
flour and shake off the excess.
2. Melt the graisse normande or butter in a heavy pot. Add the
shanks and brown on both sides over high heat.
3. Reduce the heat and add the chopped onions and the leeks.
Cover and cook for 5 minutes.

4. Add the tarragon, cider, brown stock, and bouquet garni. Bring to a boil, reduce the heat, and simmer for 1 hour and 45 minutes. If too much liquid evaporates, add water or more brown stock to just cover the shanks.

5. Transfer the meat to a serving platter and keep warm. Remove the bouquet garni and discard. Skim as much of the fat as possible from the surface of the sauce, then season to taste. This dish can be prepared ahead of time.

RIS DE VEAU BRAISÉ ARGENTAN
Braised Sweetbreads, Argentan Style

SERVES 2

1½ pounds sweetbreads
¼ cup chopped bacon
1 tablespoon flour
¼ cup carrots, peeled and
cut into ¼-inch slices
½ cup mushrooms, cleaned
and quartered

2 teaspoons chopped
shallots
½ cup dry white wine
½ cup Brown Stock (page
27)
Salt and pepper

1. In a large saucepan cover the sweetbreads with water and bring to a boil. Simmer for 5 minutes, remove the sweetbreads, and place them in cold water until they are cool. Remove all fat and membranes.

2. In a skillet fry the bacon until it renders some fat. Pour off most of the fat and lightly brown the sweetbreads on all sides. Sprinkle with the flour and continue to cook for 2 or 3 minutes.

3. Add the carrots, mushrooms, and shallots and cook another 3 or 4 minutes.

4. Stir in the white wine and brown stock, bring to a boil, reduce the heat, and simmer uncovered for 35 to 40 minutes.

5. Transfer the sweetbreads to a serving dish and season the sauce and vegetables to taste.

RIS DE VEAU GRANDMÈRE
Sweetbreads, Grandmother Style

My mother reminded me of this recipe the last time I was in Normandy. Nobody could seem to remember whether the dish had any particular name, only that my grandmother liked to prepare it. In any case, this is a wonderful recipe.

8 large cabbage leaves,
    Savoy if possible
2 pounds sweetbreads
6 tablespoons butter
½ cup carrots, peeled and
    cut into ½-inch slices
½ cup leeks (white part
    only), thinly sliced
2 tablespoons flour

½ cup cider
3 cups Brown Stock (page
    27)
Bouquet garni (1 sprig
    fresh thyme, 5 to 6
    stems parsley, and 1
    bay leaf tied between 2
    or 3 green leek leaves)
Salt and pepper

SERVES 4

1. Remove and discard the thick ribs from the cabbage leaves. Boil in 2 quarts water for 10 minutes, then cool under cold running water.
2. Cut the sweetbreads into 8 pieces and remove as much of the fat and membrane as possible.
3. Melt the butter in a large saucepan and lightly brown the sweetbreads on all sides. Reserve the butter in the pan.
4. Wrap each section of sweetbread in a cabbage leaf and fasten with a toothpick.
5. In the same pan in which you browned the sweetbreads, cook the carrots and the leeks covered for 4 or 5 minutes. Stir the flour into the pan. Continue to cook for 3 to 4 minutes.
6. Pour in the cider and the brown stock and stir well. Bring to a boil and reduce the heat. Add the bouquet garni and the sweetbreads wrapped in the cabbage leaves and simmer for 30 minutes.
7. Remove the sweetbreads. Discard the toothpicks and the bouquet garni. Season the sauce to taste and pour over the sweetbreads.

CERVELLES AU BEURRE NOIR
Calf's Brains in Brown Butter

Sweet and delicate, calf's brains are often served to children before they are old enough to eat any other meats. Lamb's brains are also quite popular, served cold in a salad or in a gratin.

SERVES 2

2 calf's brains
2 tablespoons white
 vinegar
4 tablespoons butter
Flour for dredging

1 teaspoon chopped fresh
 parsley
¼ teaspoon chopped chives
¼ teaspoon cider vinegar
Salt and pepper

1. Soak the brains overnight in cold water in the refrigerator. Remove all membranes and connective tissue from the surfaces the next day.
2. Bring 2 cups water and 2 tablespoons white vinegar to a boil and add the brains. Simmer for approximately 10 minutes. Remove the brains and place in cold water. Set aside.
3. When the brains have cooled, cut each one into 6 slices, approximately ½ inch thick. Flour each slice on both sides.
4. Melt 2 tablespoons of the butter in a skillet and sauté the slices until they are brown on both sides. Place on a platter and keep warm.
5. Add the remaining butter to the pan and brown it over medium heat. Quickly add the parsley and the chives and stir. Remove the pan from the heat and add the cider vinegar. Season to taste.
6. Pour the sauce over the brains and serve.

FOIE DE VEAU GRILLÉE
À LA BEURRÉE
Calf's Liver Broiled with Butter and Herbs

This dish is traditionally grilled over dried wood—usually apple wood—in the fireplace. If you have an outdoor grill, you may wish to try it that way. If not, simply prepare under the broiler.

8 tablespoons butter, at room temperature
2 slices calf's liver, approximately 1 pound each
1 teaspoon finely chopped shallots
1 teaspoon chopped fresh chervil or ½ teaspoon dried chevil

2 teaspoons chopped fresh parsley or 1 teaspoon dried parsley
Pinch of ground cloves
Pinch of nutmeg
½ teaspoon cider vinegar
Salt and pepper

SERVES 4

1. Melt 2 tablespoons of the butter and brush it on the liver. Place the liver on a plate and set aside at room temperature for 10 minutes.
2. In a bowl combine the remaining butter, shallots, chervil, parsley, ground cloves, nutmeg, and cider vinegar. Mix well and season to taste.
3. Place the liver slices under a hot broiler or on a grill and cook for 3 to 4 minutes. Turn the liver slices over and baste each with about 1 teaspoon of the herb butter. Cook for another 3 or 4 minutes. Remove.
4. Slice the liver on a bias into slices approximately ¼ inch thick. Arrange on an ovenproof platter. Spoon the herb butter over the liver and place the platter over the grill or under the broiler just long enough to melt the butter. Serve at once.

If you do not have a platter, simply melt the butter in a pan and pour it over the liver.   NOTE

TÊTE DE VEAU À LA NORMANDE
Calf's Head, Norman Style

The preparation for calf's head actually involves three separate elements: the skin, brain, and tongue. The skin and the tongue are simmered with fresh vegetables and herbs, while the brain is poached separately. They are then served together with a tangy vinaigrette thickened with hard-boiled eggs. Unless you have done it before, ask your butcher to bone out the head.

SERVES 8

1 calf's brain
1 calf's tongue
Skin from the head, rolled
   and tied
½ lemon
8 carrots, peeled and
   quartered
16 small potatoes, peeled

8 ribs celery, quartered
Bouquet garni (1 sprig
   fresh thyme, 5 to 6
   stems parsley, and 1
   bay leaf tied between 2
   or 3 green leek leaves)
1 teaspoon cider vinegar

Vinaigrette
2 hard-boiled eggs, finely
   chopped
½ cup finely chopped
   onions
¼ cup cider vinegar

1 teaspoon chopped fresh
   parsley
¾ cup peanut oil
Salt and pepper

1. Soak the brain and the tongue overnight in cold water in your refrigerator. Remove and discard all membranes and connective tissue from the surface of the brain. Set aside.
2. In a large pot cover the skin and the tongue with water, bring to a boil, and simmer for 20 to 25 minutes. Drain and cool under cold running water. Rub the lemon along the exposed skin and set aside. Remove all cartilage and fat from the largest section of the tongue and set aside.
3. Place the rolled and tied skin back in the large pot, cover with water, and bring to a boil. Simmer for 1 hour and 15 minutes.
4. Add the tongue, carrots, potatoes, celery, and bouquet garni to the pot and continue to simmer for 1 hour more.

5. While the skin and tongue are simmering, prepare the vinaigrette. Combine the hard-boiled eggs, onions, cider vinegar, and parsley and stir into a light paste. Gradually whisk in the peanut oil to form an emulsion. Season to taste and leave at room temperature.

6. Approximately 45 minutes after you added the tongue and vegetables to the pot, bring the brain and 1 teaspoon of the cider vinegar to a boil in enough water to completely cover in a separate saucepan. Reduce the heat and simmer for 15 minutes. Drain and slice the brain into 8 pieces. Keep warm.

7. Remove the tongue and peel it. Cut into 16 slices and keep warm.

8. Remove the skin and cut into approximately 2-inch squares.

9. Arrange the tongue, skin, and brain on a serving platter with the vegetables. Serve with the vinaigrette.

ALOYAU SAINT AMAND
Sirloin Roast with Apples and Crème Fraîche

The *aloyau* is a French cut of sirloin which in this country would include a piece of the tenderloin. You may substitute a sirloin roast, however.

SERVES 2

2 tablespoons Graisse Normande (page 21) or butter
1-pound sirloin roast, well trimmed
2 tablespoons finely chopped shallots
¼ cup carrots, peeled and cut into ¼-inch slices
1 apple (Granny Smith, Golden Delicious, or McIntosh), peeled, cored, and cut into ½ -inch cubes
¼ cup cider
1 teaspoon Calvados
¼ cup Crème Fraîche (page 23) or heavy cream
Salt and pepper

1. Melt the graisse normande in a small roasting pan and remove from the heat. Place the roast in the pan. Add the shallots and the carrots and place the pan in a preheated 400°F
oven for approximately 20 to 25 minutes.
2. Transfer the meat from the pan to a platter and keep it
warm on the back of the stove. Add the apple and the cider
to the pan and return it to the oven for 10 minutes.
3. Add the Calvados and the crème fraîche and continue to
cook for another 10 minutes.
4. Return the sirloin to the pan and cook in the oven for 5
minutes more.
5. Remove from the oven and slice the meat in thin strips. To
serve, arrange the meat on a warm platter with the carrots and
apples around it. Season the sauce to taste.

POÊLÉE DE "CHAÎ"
Skirt Steak in the Fashion of
the Calvados Master

A quick meal for the Calvados master when the brandy has
reached a critical point in the distilling process and he cannot
leave his post. A *chaî* is actually an aboveground storage room
in a winery or distillery, but in many of the smaller Calvados
distilleries, it is also the area in which the stills are located.

SERVES 2　　*1-pound beef skirt steak*　　*1 teaspoon cider vinegar*
　　　　　　Salt and pepper　　　　　　*¼ cup Brown Stock (page*
　　　　　　2 tablespoons Graisse　　　　　*27)*
　　　　　　　　Normande (page 21) or　　*1 teaspoon chopped fresh*
　　　　　　　　butter　　　　　　　　　　　*parsley*
　　　　　　¼ cup chopped onions

1. Make 4 or 5 diagonal cuts approximately ⅛ inch deep across the grain of the skirt steak. Season the meat on both sides.
2. Melt the graisse normande or butter in a skillet and sauté the steak for 5 to 6 minutes on each side over medium heat.
3. Remove the steak from the pan and keep warm.
4. Add the chopped onions to the pan and brown slightly. Finally, add the cider vinegar, beef stock, and parsley. Bring to a boil and remove from the heat. Season to taste.
5. Slice the meat thinly on a bias and serve with the sauce.

ONGLET À LA COQUEREL
Beef Tenderloin with Mushrooms, Shallots, and Calvados

This preparation is usually made with the hanging tenderloin, a cut of beef that is tastier and more tender than the tenderloin itself. You probably won't find it at your supermarket, but you may be able to get it from a butcher. If not, simply purchase tenderloin.

SERVES 4

2 tablespoons Graisse Normande (page 21) or butter
2-pound hanging tenderloin, well trimmed, or same amount of tenderloin
1 cup whole small mushrooms (if only large mushrooms are available, cut into quarters)

1 tablespoon finely chopped shallots
1 teaspoon Calvados
¼ cup Brown Stock (page 27)
Salt and pepper

1. In a skillet with a cover melt the graisse normande or butter. Add the meat and cover. Raise the heat and brown on one side for 5 to 6 minutes.
2. Turn the meat over, add the mushrooms and the shallots, cover, and continue to brown for approximately 5 minutes.
3. Pour the Calvados over the meat and let it cook uncovered for another 2 to 3 minutes. Remove the meat and cut it in half. Keep warm.
4. Add the brown stock to the pan and cook for 1 minute, stirring with a wooden spoon or spatula to dissolve the browned bits in the bottom of the pan. Season to taste and serve with the meat.

ROSETTES DE BOEUF NORMANDE
Beef Tenderloin with Mushrooms, Onions, and Crème Fraîche

Rosettes, which figuratively refer to the "red cheeks" of the country people, are actually the cut taken from the tail of the beef tenderloin. Second meanings notwithstanding, this is a quick, satisfying dish.

4 tablespoons butter
8 slices beef tenderloin, approximately ¼ pound each
¼ teaspoon finely crushed peppercorns
½ cup thinly sliced onions
¾ cup chanterelles or ordinary mushrooms, sliced

1 teaspoon Calvados
¾ cup Crème Fraîche (page 23) or heavy cream
¼ cup Brown Stock (optional; page 27)
Salt

SERVES 4

1. In a skillet melt the butter to a nutty brown color. While the butter is browning, sprinkle both sides of the tenderloin slices with the crushed peppercorns. Sauté the beef slices for 3 minutes on each side. Transfer to a platter and keep warm.
2. After all the meat has been sautéed, add the sliced onions and sauté for 2 to 3 minutes. Add the sliced mushrooms and sauté for another 3 to 4 minutes, or until they start to brown.
3. Add the Calvados, crème fraîche, and brown stock and simmer for 5 minutes more. Season with salt. Pour the sauce over the meat and serve.

BOEUF À LA MODE DE CAEN
Pot Roast, Caen Style

A hearty Norman pot roast, with the cooking liquid gelatinized and enriched by the addition of pork skin and a calf's foot. During the summertime, this dish is often served cold. Calf's feet may be found at your local butcher.

SERVES 4 TO 6

1 calf's foot
½ pound pork skin or rind
2 tablespoons Graisse Normande (page 21) or butter
3-pound boneless beef chuck roast, tied, if necessary
1 tablespoon Calvados
2 cups cider
1 cup Brown Stock (page 27) or water
2 leeks (white part only), chopped

2 carrots, peeled and cut into ¼-inch slices
1 large onion, peeled and cut into ⅛-inch slices
1 clove garlic, minced
Bouquet garni (1 sprig fresh thyme, 5 to 6 stems parsley, and 1 bay leaf tied between 2 or 3 green leek leaves)
Salt and pepper

1. Boil the calf's foot and the pork skin or rind in 2 quarts water for 10 minutes. Drain and rinse under cold running water. Roll the pork skin and tie with a string.
2. In a large pot melt the graisse normande or butter and brown the beef. Add the Calvados, cider, brown stock, calf's foot, and pork skin and bring to a boil. Reduce the heat, cover, and simmer for approximately 30 minutes.
3. Add the leeks, carrots, onion, garlic, and bouquet garni and simmer covered for 2 hours, or until the meat is tender.
4. Remove the meat, calf's foot, and pork skin. Discard the bouquet garni. Skim as much fat as possible from the liquid.
5. Remove as much meat from the foot and the skin as possible. Cut into small pieces and return to the pot. Season to taste.
6. Slice or cut the meat into serving portions and serve with the vegetables and cooking liquid.

BOEUF MARINÉ
Marinated Beef

A Norman version of German sauerbrauten. The cider and vinegar not only impart a tangy flavor to the chuck, they tenderize it as well. Plan this dish well ahead so the beef can marinate for at least 48 hours before you cook it.

*3-pound boneless beef
    chuck roast*
*3 medium onions, peeled
    and thinly sliced*
*2 cups carrots, peeled and
    cut into ½-inch slices*
4 cups cider
2 tablespoons cider vinegar
*4 tablespoons Graisse
    Normande (page 21) or
    butter*

1 tablespoon flour
*1 clove garlic, finely
    minced*
*Bouquet garni (1 sprig
    fresh thyme, 5 to 6
    stems parsley, and 1
    bay leaf tied between 2
    or 3 green leek leaves)*
½ cup heavy cream
Salt and pepper

SERVES 4

1. In a large bowl combine the meat, onions, carrots, cider, and cider vinegar. Let them marinate in the refrigerator for at least 48 hours.
2. After the meat has marinated, remove it and dry well with paper towels. Reserve the liquid and vegetables.
3. In a heavy pot melt the graisse normande or butter. Add the meat and brown it on all sides. Add the flour to the fat and stir. Cook for 2 to 3 minutes more.
4. Add the marinade with all of the vegetables, the garlic, and the bouquet garni. Bring to a boil and simmer uncovered for 10 minutes. Skim as much fat as possible from the surface of the liquid. Reduce the heat, cover, and cook for 1 hour and 30 minutes, or until the meat is tender. (At this point, the dish is usually removed from the heat, cooled, and then reheated the next day, but this is optional.)
5. Remove the meat and keep warm. Remove the bouquet

garni and discard. Add the heavy cream to the cooking liquid and simmer for 15 to 20 minutes more. Season to taste.

6. Cut the meat into serving portions and serve with the vegetables and the sauce.

DAUBE DE BOEUF
Beef Stewed in Cider
with Carrots, Leeks, and Potatoes

In the other French provinces, a daube would be simmered in a red wine, often of the particular region. Since Normandy has no wine of its own, this dish has evolved using varying amounts of cider, water, and brown stock. Water can be substituted for the brown stock, but the broth won't be as rich. We often served this dish with buttered and toasted slices of French bread.

SERVES 4 TO 6

½ pound salt pork, washed and cut into ¼-inch pieces
4-pound boneless beef chuck roast, cut into 1-inch cubes
1 clove garlic, chopped
1 leek, chopped
2 tablespoons flour
2 cups cider
3 cups Brown Stock (page 27) or water

4 large carrots, peeled and cut into ½-inch slices
Bouquet garni (1 sprig fresh thyme, 5 to 6 stems parsley, and 1 bay leaf tied between 2 or 3 green leek leaves)
4 to 6 potatoes, peeled and quartered
12 thin slices French bread
Butter
Salt and pepper

1. In a heavy pot slightly brown the salt pork over medium heat. Remove the pieces of pork and discard.

2. In the rendered pork fat, brown the beef on all sides over medium-to-high heat.

3. After the meat has browned, reduce the heat and add the chopped garlic and the leeks. Cook for 10 minutes.

4. Add the flour to the pot and stir well. Cook for another 4 to 5 minutes.

5. Pour in the cider and the brown stock and bring to a boil. Stir well. Add the carrots and the bouquet garni and simmer for 30 minutes.

6. Add the potatoes and simmer for 1 hour more, or until the meat is tender. Season to taste.

7. Just before you are about to serve the daube, butter the bread on both sides and quickly toast in a skillet. Serve with the dinner.

GRATIN DE CHOUX À LA VIANDE
Shredded Beef with Onions and Cabbage in a Cheese Sauce

There were almost always leftovers after my mother served a *pot au feu*. This dish is a tasty way of using up the beef and cabbage the next day. Shred the cooked beef in a food processor or by hand if it is not tender enough.

16 cabbage leaves
Salt and pepper
2 tablespoons butter
½ cup chopped onions

2 cups shredded boiled
*   beef*
1 tablespoon flour
¾ cup brown stock

SERVES 4

Sauce
2 tablespoons butter
1 tablespoon flour
2 cups milk
½ cup grated French
*   Emmenthaler or*
*   Gruyère cheese*

Salt and pepper

1. Bring the cabbage leaves, 1 tablespoon salt, and 2 quarts water to a boil. Simmer for 15 minutes, or until the leaves are tender. Drain and cool under cold running water. Set aside.

2. Melt the butter in a skillet. Add the onions and sauté until they begin to brown. Add the shredded beef and sauté for 4 to 5 minutes more. Sprinkle the flour over the beef and stir well. Cook for another 5 minutes, stirring constantly. Add the beef stock, stir for another 5 minutes, and season to taste.

3. In a buttered baking dish or shallow casserole, layer a few cabbage leaves along the bottom. Spoon out a layer of beef next. Repeat this layering process until you have used all the beef and cabbage leaves. Set aside.

4. To make the sauce, melt the butter in a small saucepan and add the flour. Stir well and cook for 3 to 4 minutes. Gradually pour in the milk, stirring to avoid lumps, until the sauce thickens. Remove from the heat and stir in ¼ cup of the grated cheese. Season to taste.

5. Pour the sauce over the layered cabbage and beef. Sprinkle the remaining grated cheese on top. Place in a preheated 375° F oven and bake for 45 to 60 minutes, or until lightly browned.

POT AU FEU NORMAND
Boiled Beef, Norman Style

This classic boiled beef dinner is served with a creamy horseradish sauce. It is also an excellent way of making 2 or 3 quarts of rich stock.

3-pound boneless beef chuck roast
2 pounds short ribs
2-pound beef shank, cut into 6–8 slices
Salt and pepper
3 leeks, approximately 5 inches long (white and green parts), washed, trimmed, and tied together
4 turnips, peeled and quartered
6 carrots, peeled and cut into 4 pieces each

1 small cabbage, quartered
1 celery root, peeled and quartered, or 4 ribs celery, trimmed and cut into 5 or 6 pieces each
1 large onion, peeled, halved, and studded with 1 clove in each half
Bouquet garni (1 sprig fresh thyme, 5 to 6 stems parsley, and 1 bay leaf tied between 2 or 3 green leek leaves)

SERVES 6 TO 8

Sauce
1 cup heavy cream
1 tablespoon prepared horseradish
Pinch of nutmeg

Pinch of freshly ground pepper
¼ teaspoon cider vinegar

1. Bring the chuck, short ribs, and beef shanks to a boil in 16 cups water and 1 tablespoon salt. Reduce the heat and simmer for 30 minutes. Skim the impurities from the surface.
2. Add the leeks, turnips, carrots, cabbage, celery root, onions, and bouquet garni. Simmer for 1½ to 2 hours, or until the meat is tender.
3. To make the horseradish sauce, bring the heavy cream to a boil and add the prepared horseradish, nutmeg, a pinch of pepper, and cider vinegar. Simmer for 3 to 4 minutes, remove from the heat, and keep warm.

4. Transfer the chuck roast from the broth and slice it. Arrange on a platter with the shanks and the short ribs.

5. Cut the cabbage into 8 pieces. Remove the string from the leeks and cut them into serving pieces. Cut the celery root into serving pieces. Arrange all the vegetables around the meat and serve with the sauce.

NOTE   *The cooking broth may also be served as a soup if you wish. Simply season with a little salt and pepper.*

TRIPES À LA MODE DE CAEN
Tripe, Caen Style

A true classic of Norman cookery, this dish has a history that stretches back to the time of the Viking invasions. Normans take this painstakingly prepared dish with a high degree of seriousness, to the extent that a competition is held every year in Caen to determine the finest recipe in the province. The winner is presented with the Tripière d'Or, an award in the shape of the earthenware pot in which the dish is traditionally cooked. Flat and round, the *tripière* was designed to lose as little moisture as possible during the long, slow cooking process —often 10 to 12 hours—and many cooks even seal the small opening at the top with a paste of flour and water to prevent further evaporation. The women of the towns would often bring this dish to the baker to cook in his ovens while he prepared his breads and rolls.

You will need two full days to prepare this dish since it should rest midway through the cooking process. The outcome, however, is a culinary treasure, worthy of its long celebrated history.

SERVES 5 TO 6

1 beef foot or 2 calf's feet
½ pound pork skin, well washed
5 pounds tripe, washed several times and cut into 2-inch squares
3 cups hard cider
8 cups Brown Stock (page 27) or water
3 cups carrots, peeled and thinly sliced
2 leeks (white and green parts), washed and thinly sliced

2 cups thinly sliced onions
Bouquet garni (1 bay leaf, 1 clove, 1 sprig fresh thyme or ½ teaspoon dried thyme, 1 clove garlic, crushed, and ½ teaspoon crushed black peppercorns tied in a cheesecloth bag)
1 tablespoon Calvados
1 tablespoon salt

1. In a large pot bring the beef foot or calf's feet and the pork skin to a boil in enough water to cover for 15 minutes. Drain and cool under cold running water. Remove all the meat from the foot and cut into pieces no larger than 1 inch square. Cut the pork skin into pieces of the same size.

2. In a heavy pot add the tripe, the meat from the foot, the skin, the cider, and the brown stock or water. Bring to a boil, reduce the heat to low, cover, and simmer for 5 hours. Place a weight on top of the cover so as little moisture as possible escapes. During this time, the tripe will shrink by approximately half, but the moisture level should not decrease substantially.

3. Remove from the heat and cool overnight in the refrigerator.

4. The next day slowly return the tripe to a simmer. Add the carrots, leeks, onions, and bouquet garni and simmer gently for another 5 hours.

5. Just before you remove the tripe from the heat, add the Calvados and approximately 1 tablespoon salt. The liquid will have turned a rich amber color, and the vegetables will be exceptionally sweet and tender, as will the tripe. Skim the fat from the top and discard the bouquet garni. Serve the tripe very hot with the vegetables and the broth.

LANGUE DE BOEUF
Beef Tongue with a Piquant Sauce

The tongue is often cooked with a pot au feu, then reheated and served the next day. This recipe calls for the tongue to be simmered in water, but if you have enough brown stock or perhaps broth from a pot au feu, use that; it will enhance the flavor of the tongue. The piquant sauce may be served with any boiled meat.

1 beef or veal tongue
4 carrots, peeled
4 turnips, peeled
4 leeks (white and green parts), approximately 5 inches long, washed and trimmed
Bouquet garni (1 sprig fresh thyme, 5 to 6 stems parsley, and 1 bay leaf tied between 2 or 3 green leek leaves)

1 small onion, peeled, halved, and studded with 1 clove in each half

SERVES 6

Sauce
¼ cup finely chopped onions
¼ cup cider vinegar or cornichons vinegar
¼ teaspoon crushed peppercorns
2 tablespoons butter
3 tablespoons flour
2 cups Brown Stock (page 27)

2 tablespoons finely chopped cornichons (sour gherkins)
1 teaspoon capers
1 tablespoon chopped fresh parsley
1 teaspoon chopped chives
Salt

1. In a large pot cover the tongue with water and bring to a boil. Simmer for 30 minutes, drain, and cool under cold running water. (This step can be done a day in advance.)
2. When the tongue has cooled, trim the part nearest the

throat—the largest section—of all cartilage and fat. Do not remove the skin at this point.

3. Cover the tongue completely with water and bring to a boil. Simmer for 1 hour. If too much water evaporates, add more; the tongue should remain submerged.

4. Add the carrots, turnips, leeks, bouquet garni, and onion halves. Continue to simmer for another hour, or until the tongue is fork tender.

5. Meanwhile, prepare the sauce. In a small saucepan bring the onions, cider vinegar, and crushed peppercorns to a boil. Cook over high heat until nearly all the liquid has evaporated. Remove from the heat.

6. In another saucepan melt the butter and stir in the flour. Cook for 3 or 4 minutes, then stir in the beef stock. Bring to a boil and add to the onion and vinegar mixture.

7. Add the cornichons and capers and simmer for 10 minutes. Add the parsley and the chives and remove from the heat. Season with salt to taste and keep warm.

8. When the tongue is tender, remove it from the liquid. Allow it to cool for a few minutes and then remove the skin. Cut it into serving slices and keep warm. Remove the carrots, turnips, and leeks, cut them into serving portions, and arrange around the tongue. Serve with the piquant sauce.

CARRÉ DE PORC RÔTI AU CIDRE
Rack of Pork Basted with Cider

Pigs bred in Normandy are prized for their lean high-quality meat, and the regional pork dishes are relatively free of fat. Pork loin is often roasted or even pot roasted and served with the savory cooking juices enriched with stock, wine, or, as in this recipe, cider.

2 cups cider
2 cloves
4 tablespoons butter
4-pound pork loin roast,
  cut from rib section
¼ teaspoon thyme

Salt and pepper
3 carrots, peeled and cut
  into ¼-inch cylinders
3 onions, peeled and
  coarsely chopped

SERVES 4 TO 6

1. In a saucepan bring the cider and the cloves to a boil. Remove from the heat and set aside.
2. Melt the butter in a roasting pan on top of the stove and brown the pork loin, meat side down. When it has browned, turn it over and sprinkle with the thyme and salt and pepper.
3. Place the roast in a preheated 350°F oven for 45 minutes. Baste with the cider every 15 or 20 minutes.
4. After 45 minutes, add the carrots and onions to the roasting pan. Bake the roast for 1 hour more and continue to baste with the cider, reserving ¼ cup.
5. Remove the pork from the oven and let it sit for 10 to 15 minutes before slicing. Keep warm.
6. Skim as much fat from the roasting pan as possible. Place over low heat and add the remaining ¼ cup cider. Scrape up the browned bits with a wooden spoon or a spatula. Pour into a serving bowl.
7. Slice the pork and serve with the carrots, onions, and cider-fortified cooking juices.

FRICOT DE PORC EN COCOTTE
Braised Pork with Prunes,
Carrots, Leeks, and Shallots

My father would kill at least one pig every autumn, and the meat that was not salted would be eaten quickly, usually within a week or two. This dish is a simple braising recipe that my mother prepares with prunes and whatever fresh vegetables are available at the time. Although the brown stock adds more flavor to the braising liquid, her recipe calls for water.

SERVES 4 TO 6

*4-pound pork shoulder or
  loin roast*
Salt and pepper
6 tablespoons butter
8 small shallots, peeled
*4 medium carrots, peeled
  and cut into ¼-inch
  slices*
16 prunes, with pit
*1 leek (white and green
  parts), approximately 5
  inches long, washed
  and trimmed*

*Bouquet garni (1 sprig
  fresh thyme, 5 to 6
  stems parsley, and 1
  bay leaf tied between 2
  or 3 green leek leaves)*
2 cups cider
*1 cup Brown Stock (page
  27) or water*

1. Season the roast with salt and pepper.
2. In a large casserole or pot melt the butter. Brown the roast on all sides over medium-to-high heat.
3. Add the shallots, carrots, prunes, leeks, bouquet garni, and cider. Bring to a boil, reduce the heat, cover, and simmer for approximately 1 hour and 15 minutes.
4. Add the brown stock or water, cover, and let simmer for another 15 minutes.
5. Remove the roast and slice it. Arrange on a platter surrounded by the vegetables and prunes. Discard the bouquet garni.
6. Season the braising liquid to taste.

POTÉE PAYSANNE
Potted Boiled Pork with Vegetables

A staple of peasant cookery, this dish is served in some provinces as a soup and in others as an entrée. According to French tradition, a potée is cooked in a thick earthenware pot and should include pork and cabbage. In Normandy we use petit salé pork (see Jambon au Cidre, page 199), but since that is not widely available here, substitute either rolled picnic ham, pork butt, or pork blade.

SERVES 4

1 small Savoy or white cabbage, quartered
2 pork blades, approximately 1½ pounds each, 3-pound pork butt, or 3-pound rolled picnic ham
Salt and pepper
4 large carrots, peeled and halved
6 turnips, peeled and halved
2 parsnips, peeled and halved
2 onions, peeled, halved, and studded with 1 clove in each half
16 new potatoes, with skin
1 cup Crème Fraîche (page 23)

1. Boil the quartered cabbage in 8 cups water for approximately 20 minutes. Drain and cool under cold running water.
2. In a large pot cover the pork with 16 cups water. If using fresh pork, add 2 tablespoons salt and ¼ teaspoon pepper. Otherwise do not season. Bring to a boil, reduce the heat, and simmer for 30 minutes.
3. Add the carrots, turnips, parsnips, and onions to the pork. Simmer for approximately 45 minutes.
4. Add the potatoes and the cabbage and simmer for 30 minutes more, or until the meat and all the vegetables are tender.
5. Remove the meat and slice it. Arrange on a platter with all the vegetables. Serve with the crème fraîche and a little broth to moisten.

If you wish, the broth can be seasoned and served as a soup course.

NOTE

CÔTES DE PORC NORMANDE
Baked Pork Chops
with Sautéed Apples and Cream

Apples and pork—one of the classic combinations of all times. This is a speedy dish to prepare, but if you aren't in a hurry, serve it with Gratin de Pommes de Terre (page 224).

SERVES 4

2 tablespoons butter
8 pork chops,
approximately ¼
pound each
Salt and pepper

¼ cup bread crumbs
2 Granny Smith apples,
peeled, cored, and
sliced into 4 rings each
1 cup heavy cream

1. Melt the butter in a skillet.
2. Season the pork chops with salt and pepper and quickly brown in the skillet over medium-to-high heat. Remcve the chops from the skillet and arrange in a buttered baking pan or casserole. Sprinkle with the bread crumbs.
3. In the same skillet sauté the apple rings until they begin to brown slightly. Arrange them on top of the pork chops.
4. Add the heavy cream to the skillet and bring to boil, scraping up the browned bits from the bottom of the pan. As soon as the cream comes to a boil, pour it over the pork chops and apple slices.
5. Place the pork chops and apples in a preheated 450°F oven for 10 to 15 minutes. If the cream reduces too much during cooking, add a little more. Remove from the oven and serve.

JAMBON AU CIDRE
Ham Simmered in Cider

Smoking is not a particularly popular method for preserving foods in Normandy. Usually during slaughter time in the fall the different cuts of pork are cured in brine for varying lengths of time. On the farm, however, the meat is often packed in sea salt for up to two months and desalted later in cold water. This process, which was introduced into the province by the Romans, yields a type of meat called petit salé de porc.

   This recipe calls for a petit salé ham, but as it is extremely difficult to find in this country, substitute a Virginia ham or any ham with the bone left in. A spoonful of crème fraîche is sometimes placed on the center of each ham slice at serving time.

4 cups hard or new cider	*4 to 5 peppercorns, crushed*	SERVES 4
4 large slices Virginia ham, approximately ¼ inch thick	*6 tablespoons butter*	
	¼ teaspoon cider vinegar	
1 clove	*1 tablespoon chopped fresh parsley*	

1. Bring the cider to a boil in a large pot. Add the ham slices, the clove, and the crushed peppercorns. Reduce the heat and simmer for 30 minutes.

2. Melt 4 tablespoons of the butter in a skillet. Fry the ham slices for 5 minutes on each side over medium heat. Arrange the slices on a platter and keep warm.

3. Melt the remaining butter in the skillet. Stir in the cider vinegar. Remove from the heat and pour over the ham. Sprinkle the chopped parsley over the ham and serve.

GIGOT D'AGNEAU PRÉ SALÉ
Leg of Salt Meadow Lamb

All lambs raised in Normandy carry a first-rate reputation throughout France; their pale pink flesh is lean and flavorful and deemed excellent for broiling or roasting. However, the most highly prized lambs of the province are those raised in the salt meadows of Lower Normandy, at the foot of the Benedictine Abbey of Mont-Saint-Michel. The salt in the meadow grasses deposited by the Channel tides gives the flesh a distinctive and succulent flavor that needs little enhancing during the cooking process. Consequently, most preparations involving salt meadow lamb are uncomplicated.

Since little of this type of lamb is landed on our shores, your next best bet is the meat from a very young lamb of 25 to 30 pounds. Ask your butcher to remove the hip bones, trim the fat, and tie the leg.

SERVES 6

6-pound leg of lamb
Salt and pepper
4 tablespoons butter
12 small shallots, peeled

18 small potatoes, peeled
   and quartered
2 cups Brown Stock (page
   27)

1. Season the leg with salt and pepper and place it in a roasting pan. Dot the surface with pieces of butter. Place in a preheated 400°F oven for 30 minutes.
2. Arrange the the shallots and the potatoes in the pan around the leg, and pour approximately ½ cup of the brown stock over the leg. Continue to roast for 1 hour, basting often with the pan juices.
3. Remove the lamb from the oven and let it rest for 20 minutes. Arrange the vegetables on a platter and keep warm.
4. Skim some of the fat from the roasting pan. Place the pan on the stove over medium heat and pour in the remaining stock. Simmer for a few minutes until it reduces slightly. Season to taste.
5. Slice the lamb and serve with the vegetables and pan gravy.

RAGOÛT D'AGNEAU
Lamb Stew with Turnips and Carrots

A savory stew dish for the cold months using slightly tougher cuts of lamb.

SERVES 6 TO 8

4 tablespoons Graisse Normande (page 21) or butter
4-pound lamb shoulder, cut into ¾-inch cubes
2 tablespoons flour
4 cups Brown Stock (page 27)
4 cups carrots, peeled and cut into ½-inch slices
2 cups turnips, peeled and cut into ½-inch cubes

Bouquet garni (1 sprig fresh thyme, 5 to 6 stems parsley, and 1 bay leaf tied between 2 or 3 green leek leaves)
2 cups green beans, trimmed and cut in half
2 cups potatoes, peeled and cut into ½-inch cubes
Salt and pepper

1. Melt the graisse normande or butter in a heavy pot. Add the lamb and brown on all sides over high heat.
2. Sprinkle the flour over the lamb and cook for 2 or 3 minutes more, stirring well. Add the brown stock and stir until it comes to a boil. Reduce the heat and simmer for 5 minutes.
3. Add the carrots, turnips, and bouquet garni and continue to simmer for 45 minutes.
4. While the stew is simmering, bring the green beans to a boil in enough water to cover and cook for 2 minutes. Drain and cool the beans under cold running water. Set aside.
5. After 45 minutes add the potatoes to the stew and continue to simmer for 15 minutes.
6. Add the green beans and simmer for another 15 minutes. Remove the bouquet garni. Season the stew to taste and serve.

CÔTELETTES D'AGNEAU GRILLÉES À LA SAUCE AIGRE
Lamb Chops in a Sour Sauce

A delicious way to prepare tender spring lamb. Serve with Flageolets au Beurre (page 217) and Gratin de Pommes de Terre (page 224).

2 tablespoons walnut or peanut oil
1 clove garlic, finely minced
1 teaspoon chopped savory
1 teaspoon finely crushed peppercorns

16 lamb chops, from the rack and loin, well trimmed
Salt

SERVES 4

Sauce
1 tablespoon chopped shallots
1 teaspoon crushed peppercorns
2 tablespoons cider vinegar

½ cup cider
1 cup Brown Stock (page 27)
4 tablespoons butter
Salt and pepper

1. In a bowl combine the walnut or peanut oil, garlic, savory, and crushed peppercorns. Mix well and let sit at room temperature for at least 15 minutes.

2. Lightly brush the lamb chops with the oil mixture and then set them aside while you prepare the sauce.

3. To prepare the sauce, combine the shallots, peppercorns, and cider vinegar in a small saucepan. Bring to a boil and cook until almost dry. Add the cider and continue to boil for 3 to 4 minutes.

4. Add the brown stock, reduce the heat, and simmer the sauce for 25 to 30 minutes.

5. Approximately 10 minutes before the sauce is done simmering, salt the lamb chops lightly and brown under a hot broiler for 3 to 4 minutes on each side, or until they are cooked to your

taste. Arrange on a platter. Remove sauce from the heat, and stir in the butter and salt and pepper to taste. Serve with the lamb chops.

LAPIN À LA MOUTARDE
Roast Rabbit Basted with Mustard and Butter

SERVES 4

4-pound rabbit, skinned and dressed, with liver
4 tablespoons butter, melted
¼ cup Dijon-style mustard
Salt and pepper

1 tablespoon Calvados
¼ cup cider
1 cup Crème Fraîche (page 23)
1 teaspoon butter

1. Remove then chop approximately 2 tablespoons of fat from inside the cavity of the rabbit, chop finely, and reserve. Wash and dry the rabbit completely with paper towels and arrange in a roasting pan with the chopped fat.
2. Brush the rabbit with 1 tablespoon of the melted butter and mix the remaining 3 tablespoons butter with the mustard. Season the rabbit lightly and place in a preheated 425°F oven for 20 minutes. Baste the rabbit 2 or 3 times with the rendered fat and butter.
3. After 20 minutes remove the rabbit and brush with the mustard-and-butter mixture. Return to the oven and reduce the temperature to 350°F. Repeat the basting procedure every 10 or 15 minutes for 1 hour and 30 minutes, or until you run out of the mustard-and-butter.
4. Remove the rabbit from the roasting pan and keep it warm while you make the sauce.
5. To make the sauce, place the roasting pan on the stove over medium heat and add the Calvados and cider. Simmer for 5 minutes until the liquid has reduced to almost dry.
6. Add the crème fraîche and stir with a wooden spoon, dissol-

ving the browned bits from the bottom of the pan. Simmer for 4 to 5 minutes. Season to taste and strain through cheesecloth into a serving bowl. Keep warm.

7. Melt 1 teaspoon butter in a skillet and sauté the liver for 4 to 5 minutes. Cut into as many pieces as there are people eating and serve with the rabbit.

8. To serve the rabbit, first cut it in half lengthwise, then into quarters. Serve with the sauce.

LAPIN AUX PRUNEAUX
Stewed Rabbit with Prunes

Rabbits are so large in Normandy that usually only the hind half is used to make this stew. Most farmers—my father included—raise their own rabbits for meat, much as they would raise ducks or sheep, although wild rabbits are also used in these preparations.

1 pound prunes, drained and pitted
4-pound rabbit, skinned and dressed, with liver and kidneys, cut into 8 pieces
Flour for dredging, plus 1 tablespoon for the sauce
4 tablespoons butter
¼ cup chopped onions
1 teaspoon cider vinegar

1 cup dry red wine
2 cups Brown Stock (page 27)
Bouquet garni (1 sprig fresh thyme, 5 to 6 stems parsley, and 1 bay leaf tied between 2 or 3 green leek leaves)
1 clove garlic, minced
Salt and pepper

SERVES 4

1. Pour 2 cups boiling water over the prunes and let them stand.

2. Trim a little fat from the rabbit and reserve. Dredge the pieces in flour, shaking off the excess.

3. Melt the butter in a heavy pot. Place the floured pieces of rabbit in the pot and brown slightly on all sides.

4. Add the chopped onions and sauté for 3 to 4 minutes in the butter. Sprinkle 1 tablespoon of the flour into the butter, stir, and cook for 4 to 5 minutes.

5. Add the cider vinegar and the dry red wine, bring to a boil, and stir. Add the brown stock, bouquet garni, and garlic. Cover the pot and simmer for 30 minutes.

6. In a small saucepan render a little of the rabbit fat, then add the liver and kidneys. Sauté for 5 or 6 minutes.

7. Add the prunes, liver, and kidneys to the stew and simmer for 30 minutes. Season to taste and serve.

SELLE DE CHEVREUIL
À LA CRÈME
Saddle of Venison with Crème Fraîche

Basting with crème fraîche is an old Norman technique used when roasting or broiling cuts of meat containing little of their own fat. The crème fraîche not only forms a seal to help the meat retain more of its natural moisture and flavor, but it becomes an important element of the sauce as well. This technique can be applied to veal and pork roasts and even large chicken or turkey breasts.

SERVES 7 TO 8

2 tablespoons of butter
5- to 6-pound venison
*   saddle, tied*
Salt and pepper
4 shallots

2 cups Crème Fraîche (page 23)
½ cup Brown Stock (page 27) or water
1 teaspoon cider vinegar

1. Place a roasting pan on the stove over a medium heat, and melt the butter in it. Lightly brown the venison roast on all sides.

2. Season the roast with salt and pepper and add the shallots to the pan. Roast for 10 minutes in a preheated 425°F oven.

3. Remove from the oven and brush or baste the roast with the crème fraîche. Continue to cook the venison for 1 hour, basting with crème fraîche every 10 minutes. Reserve ½ cup crème fraîche for the sauce.

4. Remove the roast from the pan and place it on a rack to drain.

5. Meanwhile, place the roasting pan on the stove again over a medium-to-high heat. Add the brown stock or water and vinegar, bring to a boil, and scrape the bottom of the pan with a wooden spoon to dissolve the browned bits of cooked meat. Simmer for 5 minutes.

6. Remove the shallots. Add the remaining crème fraîche, stir, and simmer for 3 or 4 minutes. Remove from the stove and strain through a cheesecloth into a serving bowl. Season to taste.

7. Slice the venison saddle and serve with the sauce.

Vegetables

We rarely needed to shop in Saint Hilaire-du-Harcouet for vegetables or herbs. For as long as I can recall, from late spring through midautumn, my mother's kitchen garden was our unfailing source of fresh produce, often yielding more during its growing season than the family could consume all year. Tight neat rows of leeks, shallots, turnips, onions, salsify, and carrots were mustered along one side of the large garden plot, while pale yellow pumpkins and stringy vines of green beans and peas sprawled along the low stone wall that defined the opposite edge. Leafy heads of romaine lettuce and chicory commanded the wide center aisles, along with stout cauliflowers and cabbages. Off to one small corner of the garden were the herbs—chervil, parsley, tarragon, and thyme—and across the fence from them, settled into their own sovereign patch of garden, were row upon row of potatoes. By the middle of July it would take a well-developed sense of balance to tread through the crowded furrows without stepping on something.

When the weather began to change during the closing weeks of the summer, my mother would start to put up jars of vegetables for the cold months. Green beans, peas, salsify, and carrots would first be cooked, then placed in jars and stacked away on shelves in the cellar next to wooden crates of potatoes, shallots, and onions. The pumpkins would be puréed or made into a sweet, spicy jam, and the herbs would be hung up to dry in a cool, dark place.

Norman vegetable dishes vary widely, depending upon the season or the dish they will accompany. Planned as a foil to rich, complex meat, poultry, or fish preparations, a vegetable may simply be boiled or sautéed and served with butter or crème fraîche. Or they may be the focal point of the meal, building their own complexity with the addition of a cheese or egg sauce, spices and herbs, fruit, meat, or a variety of other fresh vegetables.

There is great variation among mixed salads, as well, from the simple red cabbage and apple salad to a cold mixed salad of lettuces, fruits, and nuts flavored with a creamy vinaigrette heightened with mustard.

The potato is also now included in countless recipes across the province, although it has been cultivated in Normandy only since the beginning of the nineteenth century. Preparations include warm slices of potato in salads, layered hot in a gratin flavored with cream and garlic, sliced and fried with bacons and onions, grated and pressed into pancakes and then fried in graisse normande, or formed into potato dumplings and served with numerous accompaniments.

ASPERGES À LA SAUCE AUX OEUFS
Asparagus with an Egg Sauce

A superb appetizer or accompaniment. The egg sauce is something of a bourgeoise hollandaise and perhaps even its forerunner. I learned to make this egg sauce while an apprentice in Normandy and did not change to a more classical hollandaise until I moved to Paris. Although the same technique is applied in the preparation, the flavor is somewhat different; considerably less butter is incorporated into this sauce—only about one-third as much—and it is finished with cider vinegar instead of the more elegant lemon juice.

1½ pounds fresh asparagus   SERVES 4

Sauce
3 egg yolks   *⅛ teaspoon cider vinegar*
8 tablespoons butter, at   *Salt and pepper*
*   room temperature*

1. Trim off the tough ends of the aparagus and then peel off the tough skin with a small, sharp knife to within 2 to 3 inches of the top. Tie the stalks with string into bunches of 10 to 12.
2. To make the sauce, heat water in the bottom of a double boiler until it comes to a simmer. Reduce the heat to low and place the top on the double boiler. Add the egg yolks and 3 teaspoons water. Whisk until the yolks begin to thicken and

turn lemon-colored. Whisk in approximately 1 tablespoon of the butter until it has been absorbed into the yolks. Continue until all the butter has been incorporated. Remove from the heat, stir in the cider vinegar, and season to taste. Set aside.
3. Bring approximately 2 to 3 quarts water and 1 tablespoon salt to a boil. Add the asparagus and continue to boil for 5 minutes, or until tender. Drain, cut the string, and serve with the egg sauce. In Normandy the asparagus spears are dipped into the sauce, but you can also spoon the sauce over the spears before serving.

CAROTTES À LA CRÈME
Carrots in Cream

Delicious with fish and pork dishes. Purchase the smaller California carrots if they are available.

SERVES 4 TO 6

4 to 5 cups carrots, peeled and cut into ½-inch slices
2 tablespoons butter
1 teaspoon salt

1 cup Crème Fraîche (page 23) or heavy cream
Pinch of nutmeg
1 teaspoon chopped fresh parsley

1. Bring the sliced carrots to a boil in ½ cup water, to which the butter and the salt have been added. Boil approximately 15 minutes (the water will have evaporated), or until tender.
2. Add the Crème Fraîche or heavy cream and the nutmeg and cook for another 5 minutes.
3. Sprinkle with the chopped parsley and serve.

PURÉE DE CELERIS AUX POMMES
Purée of Celeriac and Apples

A light, delicious purée. Serve it with a hearty roast beef or
venison.

SERVES 6 TO 8

2 tablespoons flour
2 tablespoons milk
Salt and pepper
4 cups celeriac or celery
    root, washed, peeled,
    and cut into 1-inch
    pieces
4 tablespoons butter

3 apples (Granny Smith,
    Golden Delicious, or
    McIntosh), peeled,
    cored, and cut into
    1-inch pieces
Pinch of nutmeg
1 teaspoon sugar (optional)

1. Bring approximately 2 quarts water, the flour, milk, and 1
teaspoon salt to a boil. Add the pieces of celeriac and simmer
for 35 to 40 minutes or until tender. Drain and purée in a food
mill, food processor, or a blender. Keep warm.
2. Melt the butter in a skillet and sauté the apples for approximately 5 to 10 minutes over low heat. Purée and add to the
celeriac.
3. Add the nutmeg and the sugar, mix well, and season to
taste.

CHAMPIGNONS ROSÉS AUX HERBES
Mushrooms Sautéed with Shallots, Garlic, and Herbs

Mushrooms grow wild in the meadows and on the sides of the hills surrounding our farm, and one of us would go out with a basket and gather them just before a meal. The best mushrooms were always those that were snow white on top and slightly pink under the gills—hence the "rosé" in the title.

SERVES 4

6 tablespoons butter
1 tablespoon finely chopped shallots
1½ pounds mushrooms, cleaned, trimmed, and quartered
2 teaspoons chopped fresh parsley

1 teaspoon chopped chives
1 teaspoon chopped chervil
1 clove garlic, finely chopped
Salt

1. Melt the butter in a skillet. Add the shallots and sauté for 1 minute.
2. Add the mushrooms and sauté over medium heat for 5 minutes, stirring occasionally.
3. Add the parsley, chives, chervil, and garlic and sauté for 1 to 2 minutes more. Salt, mix well, and serve.

MORILLES AUX ÉCHALOTES
Morels with Shallots and Cream, Served on Toasted Norman Bread

This recipe calls for fresh morels, but you can substitute any fresh mushrooms. Although often served as an appetizer, Morilles aux Échalotes makes a superb side dish for roasted poultry or game.

3 tablespoons butter
2 teaspoons finely chopped
    shallots
1 pound morels, cleaned,
    trimmed, and halved
1 cup heavy cream or
    Crème Fraîche (page
    23)

Salt and pepper
4 slices Pain Brié (page
    273) or 12 slices good
    French bread

SERVES 4

1. Melt 1 tablespoon of the butter in a skillet. Add the shallots and sauté for 2 minutes.
2. Add the morels and sauté for 1 to 2 minutes, then cover and cook for 5 minutes more.
3. Pour the heavy cream or crème fraîche over the morels and simmer for approximately 10 minutes. Season with salt and pepper.
4. While the morels are cooking, spread the remaining butter on both sides of the bread. Toast in a skillet for a few minutes on both sides until golden brown.
5. Place the toast on the plates and pour the morel and cream sauce over them.

CHOU-FLEUR AU GRATIN
Cauliflower Baked with a Cheese Sauce

A rich vegetable dish for a cool fall evening. Norman cooks often include a regional semisoft cheese called La Fanière in dishes such as this, but it is unlikely that you'll find any in this country. Substitute Port Salut, Bonbel, or French Emmenthaler.

SERVES 6

*1 medium cauliflower,
   washed and trimmed
2 tablespoons milk
2 tablespoons flour
Salt
2 cups Sauce à la Crème
   pour Légumes (page
   35)*

*¾ cup grated Port Salut,
   Bonbel, or French
   Emmenthaler cheese*

1. Trim the cauliflower and leave whole.
2. In a large pot bring 2 quarts water, the milk, flour, and 1 tablespoon salt to a boil. Add the cauliflower, reduce the heat, and simmer for 25 to 30 minutes. It should remain a little underdone.
3. Meanwhile, warm the cream sauce and add the grated cheese off the heat.
4. Remove the cauliflower from the cooking liquid and break into florets. Arrange them in the bottom of a casserole or small baking pan and cover with the cheese sauce. Bake in a preheated 350°F oven for 20 to 25 minutes, or until the sauce begins to brown.

FLAGEOLETS AU BEURRE
Flageolet Beans with Onions, Carrots, and Butter

Flageolet beans are available in cans, but you are more likely to find them dried. They are a good accompaniment for broiled lamb chops.

1 pound dried flageolet beans	*1 bay leaf*	SERVES 6
2 ounces pork skin	*1 clove garlic*	
1 small onion, peeled, halved, and studded with 1 clove in each half	*1 small carrot, peeled*	
	6 tablespoons butter	
	Salt and pepper	

1. Soak the beans overnight in cold water. Drain and add the beans to 2 quarts boiling salted water. Reduce the heat and simmer for 15 minutes, skimming often.
2. Add the pork skin, onion, bay leaf, garlic, and carrot, and simmer for 1 hour, or until beans are tender.
3. Remove the onion, discarding the cloves, and the garlic and purée in a food mill or processor. Slice the pork skin into thin strips. Cut the carrot in ¼-inch slices.
4. Drain the beans, reserving 1 cup cooking liquid. In a saucepan add the butter to the liquid and bring to a boil. Add the onion-and-garlic purée, carrot, pork skin, and beans. Simmer for 1 or 2 minutes, season to taste, and serve.

HARICOTS VERTS D'ISIGNY
Green Beans, Isigny Style

French green beans, or *aiguilles,* are considerably smaller and thinner than those raised in the United States, so choose the smallest, tenderest green beans you can find. Fresh beans will snap when broken.

SERVES 4

1 pound green beans
Salt
4 tablespoons butter

1 teaspoon chopped shallots
Pepper

1. Wash the beans and cut off the stem and tip ends.
2. Bring 2 quarts water and 1 tablespoon salt to a boil. Add the green beans and boil uncovered for 3 to 4 minutes, or until the beans are cooked to your taste. Drain and keep warm.
3. While the green beans are still cooking, melt the butter in a saucepan, add the chopped shallots, and sauté for 1 minute. Add the drained green beans, toss once or twice in the butter, and remove from the heat. Season to taste and serve.

NOTE

If you prefer to boil the green beans earlier in the day and add them to the butter just before you are about to serve them, drain and then cool completely under cold running water. Place them in the refrigerator until you are ready to dress them.

LAITUES BRAISÉES SIMONE
Braised Lettuce with Mushrooms, Shallots, Hard-boiled Eggs, and Cream

This dish can be served with Sauce à la Crème pour Légumes (page 35) or by itself.

4 small heads Boston
   lettuce, washed, dried,
   and trimmed
Salt
1 tablespoon Graisse
   Normande (page 21) or
   butter
1 tablespoon finely chopped
   shallots

½ cup minced mushrooms
1 tablespoon heavy cream
Pepper
1 hard-boiled egg, coarsely
   chopped
1 cup Brown Stock (page
   27)

SERVES 4

1. Add the heads of lettuce to a large pot of boiling salted water. Simmer for 3 to 4 minutes, drain, and let the lettuce cool in a colander.

2. Melt the graisse normande or butter in a skillet. Add the shallots and sauté for 1 minute. Add the mushrooms and cook for 2 to 3 minutes more, or until the moisture has evaporated.

3. Add the heavy cream, cook for 1 minute, and season to taste.

4. Add the chopped hard-boiled egg and stir. Remove from the heat and set aside.

5. Slice each head of lettuce in half lengthwise. Divide the cream-and-egg mixture equally among the 8 halves, placing some in the center of each half.

6. Fold the lettuce in half from the tip to the core so the stuffing will be enclosed. Roll in slightly along each side. You can tie each half with string, but this is not necessary.

7. In a large pot bring the brown stock to a boil. Place each stuffed lettuce half in the liquid, reduce the heat, cover, and simmer for 20 minutes. Remove the lettuce, untie the string, and serve.

NAVETS BRAISÉS
Braised Turnips

An excellent accompaniment for stewed rabbit or beef. Use small to medium turnips.

SERVES 4 TO 6

8 turnips, peeled and cut into 8 orangelike segments
2 tablespoons Graisse Normande (page 21) or butter
1 teaspoon sugar (optional)
1 cup Brown Stock (page 27)

4 tablespoons salt pork, washed and cut into short thin strips, or coarsely chopped bacon
Salt and pepper

1. In a large saucepan bring the turnips to a boil in 1 cup water, along with the graisse normande or butter and the sugar. Continue to boil uncovered over high heat until the water has evaporated.
2. Add the brown stock, salt pork strips, and a little salt and pepper. Bring to a boil, reduce the heat, and simmer for 20 to 25 minutes. The stock will reduce during that time and cling to the turnips. Remove from the heat and serve.

PETITS POIS À LA FERTÉ-MACÉ
Fresh Peas with Lettuce, Ham, and Crème Fraîche

Small sweet peas are grown around the town of La Ferté-Macé in Lower Normandy and sold every Thursday in its farmers' market. However, the town's gastronomic reputation actually rests on a local dish called tripes en brochettes, or tripe cooked on skewers.

SERVES 4 TO 6

2 tablespoons butter
1 small head Boston lettuce,
   washed and sliced into
   thin strips (this should
   yield approximately 2
   cups)
3 cups fresh peas
2 thin slices ham, sliced
   into thin strips
½ cup Crème Fraîche (page
   23) or heavy cream
Salt and pepper

1. Melt the butter in a saucepan. Add the lettuce, stir, cover, and cook over low heat for 2 or 3 minutes.
2. Add the peas and the ham, cover, and continue to cook for 15 minutes.
3. Finally, add the crème fraîche or heavy cream and cook uncovered for 10 minutes. Season to taste and serve.

POMMES DE TERRE AU LARD
Potatoes Fried with Bacon and Onions

This simple dish is good for breakfast, lunch, or dinner. The traditional recipe calls for salt pork rather than bacon, but either is fine.

SERVES 6

4 cups potatoes, peeled,
   washed, and cut into
   ½-inch cubes
6 tablespoons butter
¾ cup coarsely chopped
   bacon or salt pork,
   washed and cut into ¼
   -inch strips
¼ cup coarsely chopped
   onions
1 tablespoon chopped fresh
   parsley
Salt and pepper

1. Place the cubed potatoes in a pot with enough cold water to cover. Bring to a boil and remove from the heat. Drain the potatoes in a colander.

2. Melt the butter in a large skillet until it begins to brown. Add the potatoes and cook over medium heat for approximately 5 minutes.

3. Add the bacon and the onions and continue to cook until the potatoes become brown and crusty. Add the parsley and season to taste.

POMMES DE TERRE EN SALADE
Warm Potato Salad

This is delicious served as a warm appetizer or with sausage or sliced boudin noir for a light lunch.

SERVES 6

⅛ cup thinly sliced bacon
*   or salt pork*
2 pounds or 25 to 30 new
*   potatoes*
Salt
2 tablespoons cider vinegar
1 teaspoon chopped chives

1 teaspoon Dijon-style
*   mustard*
1 tablespoon finely chopped
*   onions*
⅓ cup peanut oil
Freshly ground pepper

1. Brown the bacon or salt pork in a pan and set aside.

2. Boil the potatoes in enough salted water to cover for approximately 20 minutes, or until tender. Drain in a colander and let cool at room temperature. When they have cooled enough to handle, peel and cut into ¼-inch slices.

3. In a large bowl combine the cider vinegar, chives, mustard, and onions. Gradually add the oil and whisk vigorously into an emulsion.

4. Add the potatoes and bacon and toss. Season to taste. Let marinate for 30 minutes at room temperature before serving.

POMMES DE TERRE FARCIES
Potatoes Stuffed with Beef, Onions, and Bread Crumbs

A great way to use leftover boiled beef or stew. This can be served as an entrée for a light supper.

4 large baking potatoes, peeled and cut in half lengthwise
1 tablespoon Graisse Normande (page 21) or butter
¼ cup chopped onions
2 cups shredded boiled beef or the meat from beef stew

1 egg, lightly beaten
2 tablespoons dry bread crumbs
Salt and pepper
1½ cups Brown Stock (page 27)

SERVES 4

1. With a spoon carefully remove approximately ½ the flesh from each potato half. Coarsely chop the removed portion.
2. Melt the graisse normande or butter in a skillet and sauté the onions and the chopped potatoes over medium heat until light brown.
3. Add the leftover shredded beef to the skillet and toss well with the onions and potatoes. Transfer the mixture to a large bowl.
4. Add the egg and bread crumbs to the bowl and mix well. Season to taste.
5. Divide the stuffing among the hollowed-out potato halves. Arrange the potatoes in a large baking pan or casserole. Pour the brown stock around the potatoes and place in a preheated 350°F oven for 1 hour. Baste every 15 minutes with the stock. Remove and serve.

GALETTE DE POMMES DE TERRE
Potato Pancakes

In Normandy these pancakes are made the width of the skillet and then served in wedge-shaped slices. You can make the pancakes as large or as small as you wish, keeping in the mind, however, that the thicker they are, the longer they will need to cook. I try to keep the pancakes approximately ¼ inch thick.

SERVES 2 TO 4

2 cups grated potatoes
1 egg
Salt and pepper

2 tablespoons Graisse Normande (page 21) or butter

1. After you have grated the potatoes, place them in a fine strainer and press out as much liquid as possible.
2. In a bowl beat the egg with the salt and pepper. Add the grated potato and mix well.
3. Melt the graisse normande or butter in a skillet. Add the potato mixture and smooth out into pancakes ¼ inch thick. Reduce the heat and cook for approximately 5 minutes on each side, or until they brown. Serve hot.

GRATIN DE POMMES DE TERRE
Gratin of Potatoes and Cream

SERVES 6 TO 8

1 clove garlic, crushed
2 pounds or 8 medium potatoes, peeled and cut into ⅛-inch slices

Nutmeg
Salt
1½ cups heavy cream

1. Rub the crushed garlic clove around the inside of a large casserole or ovenproof dish.
2. Make a layer of potato slices along the bottom of the dish. Lightly sprinkle with the nutmeg and the salt. Repeat this process until all the potatoes are used up.

3. Bring the heavy cream to a boil, then pour it over the layered potatoes.

4. Bake uncovered in a preheated 375°F oven for 45 minutes. Cover and bake for 15 minutes more.

5. Remove the dish from the oven and let it rest for 5 to 10 minutes before serving.

QUENELLES DE POMMES DE TERRE
Potato Dumplings

After the dumplings have been poached, there are a few different methods for finishing them. I have included three.

1 pound or 4 medium potatoes, washed and peeled
Salt
8 tablespoons butter

Pinch of nutmeg
¾ cup plus 2 tablespoons flour
3 eggs

SERVES 6

1. Bring the potatoes to a boil in enough salted water to cover. Simmer 20 to 30 minutes, or until fork tender. Drain in a colander and let rest for a few minutes.

2. In a large saucepan over a low heat mash the potatoes by hand or with an electric hand mixer until smooth. Set aside and keep warm.

3. In another saucepan bring to a boil 1 cup water, ½ teaspoon salt, the butter, and the nutmeg. Add the flour and stir until smooth; this should take approximately 2 to 3 minutes. Remove from the heat and add the eggs one at a time, mixing well.

4. Add the potatoes, mix well, and let cool.

5. Bring 16 cups water and 1 tablespoon salt to a boil, then reduce the heat, and simmer.

6. There are a few ways of molding the quenelles. Probably

the easiest is simply to take approximately 2 tablespoons of the mixture and slip it into the hot water. Another method is to lightly flour a board or table and roll 2 tablespoons of the mixture into an oval shape with your hands. The third and most complex is the method used in classical kitchens to make *quenelles de brochet,* or pike quenelles. First, fill a tablespoon with the potato mixture. Then dip another tablespoon into a pot of hot water and roll the quenelle from the first tablespoon to the second, forming a smooth oval shape slightly pointed on either end. Finally use the first tablespoon to gently push the quenelle into the hot water you are going to poach it in. The last method yields elegantly shaped quenelles, but in a farmhouse kitchen either the first or second method would be used.

7. Poach 5 or 6 quenelles at a time in the hot salted water for about 10 minutes, or until they float to the top. Remove from the water and set aside. Repeat until all the mixture has been used.

8. From this point on, the choice is yours:

AU BEURRE

FOR 18
QUENELLES
6 tablespoons butter
¼ teaspoon salt

In a large skillet melt the butter with 2 tablespoons water and the salt. Add the quenelles, making sure they are not touching. Cover and simmer over low heat for 8 to 10 minutes. Serve with stew or fish.

À LA CRÈME

FOR 18
QUENELLES
1 cup Crème Fraîche (page
*　21)*
Salt and pepper to taste

Bring the crème fraîche and salt and pepper to a boil in a large shallow pot. Add the quenelles, cover, and simmer for 10 minutes.

AU GRATIN

FOR 18
QUENELLES

1 cup Sauce à la Crème
    pour Légumes (page
    35)
½ cup grated Port Salut or
    French Emmenthaler
    cheese

1. In an ovenproof dish arrange the quenelles and cover them with the cream sauce.
2. Sprinkle the grated cheese on top. Bake in a preheated 375° F oven for 25 to 30 minutes, or until lightly browned. This recipe makes an excellent appetizer.

NOQUES

A very old preparation that has been made in Normandy since the Middle Ages. Many will recognize it as being in the same family as Alsatian spaetzli or Italian gnocchi. Serve with veal or fish dishes or almost any dish that includes a cream sauce.

SERVES 8

3 eggs
2 ¼ cups flour
1 teaspoon chopped fresh
    parsley
Pinch of nutmeg

Salt
1 cup heavy cream
4 tablespoons butter
White pepper

1. Beat the eggs in a large bowl. Add the flour, parsley, nutmeg, ¼ teaspoon salt, and approximately ⅓ cup of the heavy cream. Mix together. Add another ⅓ cup cream and continue to mix. Pour in the remaining cream and mix for a few seconds until smooth.
2. Bring 1 gallon salted water to a boil. Place 1 cup noque mixture into a colander with large holes (a food mill or spaetzli

maker will also work well). Then, with a rubber spatula, press the mixture through the holes so that it drops into the boiling water. The noques will rise to the surface. When the water comes back to a boil, remove them with a slotted spoon or strainer and set aside. Continue the process until all the mixture has been used.

3. Melt the butter in a skillet. Add the noques and toss over medium heat for 2 or 3 minutes. Remove from the heat and season to taste.

SALSIFIS AU BEURRE
Salsify Browned in Butter with Onions and Mint

Salsify is available throughout the province during the late spring and well into midsummer, but according to the green grocers, never in large enough quantities. Normans love salsify and clear the market shelves within days of a delivery, preparing it, for the most part, in the manner I have indicated here —simply and with few extra elements to mask the delicate flavor. The addition of milk and flour to the cooking liquid helps the salsify to retain its color and, more importantly, its natural sweetness.

SERVES 6

2 pounds salsify or oyster plant
2 tablespoons milk
2 tablespoons flour
Salt

4 tablespoons butter
¼ cup thinly sliced onions
1 teaspoon chopped fresh mint

1. Peel the salsify. (If you have gloves, wear them; salsify will stain your hands.)
2. In a large pot bring to a boil 8 cups water, the milk, flour, and salt. Add the salsify, reduce the heat, and simmer for 45

minutes, or until tender. Drain and allow to cool. Cover with a clean damp cloth.

3. Slice the salsify into 2-inch pieces.

4. Melt the butter in a large skillet and add the salsify. Brown on all sides to a nutty color. Add the thinly sliced onions and cook until tender. Add the chopped mint, season to taste, stir, and serve.

POIVREAUX EN BLANQUETTE
Leeks in a Cream Sauce

A perfect accompaniment for game dishes.

4 tablespoons butter	*Pinch of nutmeg*	SERVES 4
3 cups leeks (white part only), cut into ½-inch slices	*1 cup Sauce à la Crème pour Légumes (page 35)*	
1 teaspoon sugar (optional)		

1. Melt the butter in a large saucepan. Add the sliced leeks and sugar and cover. Cook over low heat for 15 minutes, stirring often.

2. Add the nutmeg and the cream sauce, bring to a boil, quickly reduce the heat, and simmer uncovered for 5 minutes more. Adjust seasoning if necessary.

JARDINIÈRE DE LÉGUMES
Fresh Mixed Vegetables in Cream

A delicious mélange of fresh vegetables, often reserved for Sunday night dinners.

SERVES 8

1 teaspoon salt
1 cup new potatoes, the size of walnuts, or 1 cup larger potatoes, peeled and cut into 1-inch cubes
1 cup carrots, peeled and cut into 2- by ¼- by ¼-inch sticks, approximately
1 cup turnips, peeled and cut into 2- by ¼- by ¼-inch sticks, approximately

1 cup cauliflower, broken into florets
1 cup celery, cut into 2- by ¼- by ¼-inch sticks, approximately
½ cup fresh peas
4 tablespoons butter
1 cup heavy cream
Pinch of nutmeg
Salt and pepper

1. In a large pot bring 8 cups water and 1 teaspoon salt to a boil. Add the potatoes and cook for 5 minutes over medium heat.
2. Add the carrots and cook for 5 minutes more.
3. Add the turnips, cauliflower, and celery and cook for 7 minutes more.
4. Add the peas, cook for an additional 3 to 4 minutes, and drain.
5. In the same pot bring the butter, heavy cream, and nutmeg to a boil. Transfer all the vegetables back in and simmer for 4 to 5 minutes. Season to taste.

SALADE DE CHOUX ROUGES
Red Cabbage and Apple Salad

An uncomplicated salad that goes well with pâté or any cold food.

2 tablespoons cider vinegar
1 teaspoon sugar
1 teaspoon salt
¼ teaspoon crushed black
    peppercorns

4 cups shredded red
    cabbage
2 apples (Golden Delicious
    or McIntosh), peeled
    and cored

SERVES 4 TO 6

1. In a large pot bring to a boil ¼ cup water, the cider vinegar, sugar, salt, and pepper. Add the cabbage, bring back to a boil, and remove from the heat. Pour into a bowl, toss, and let rest for 10 minutes at room temperature.
2. Meanwhile, cut the apple in 8 pieces, then cut into ⅛-inch slices.
3. Drain off approximately ½ the liquid in the bowl, discard, and add the apples. Mix well and let rest for 1 hour. The salad may also be served immediately.

SALADE CURICHOISE
Potato Salad with Ham, Celery,
and Cream

This rich summer salad is marvelous when accompanied with smoked or cold poached fish. To vary, add chopped hard-boiled eggs.

1½ *pounds small potatoes*
2 *tablespoons cider vinegar*
Salt and pepper
1 *teaspoon Dijon-style*
    mustard
¾ *cup Crème Fraîche (page*
    23) or heavy cream

1 *cup celery, strings*
    removed and cut into
    ¼-inch slices
2 *slices ham, sliced into*
    thin strips

SERVES 4 TO 6

1. Boil the potatoes with the skins on in enough water to cover and 1 tablespoon salt. (Do not overcook; the potatoes should remain firm enough to slice when cooled.) After they have

cooked, remove them from the water, and let cool to room temperature.

2. Cut the potatoes into ¼-inch slices while still slightly warm.

3. In a large bowl combine the cider vinegar, salt and pepper, and mustard and stir. Gradually add the crème fraîche or heavy cream, whisking slowly for 2 to 3 minutes.

4. Add the sliced potatoes, celery, and ham and mix well. Adjust seasoning if necessary.

SALADE CRESSON AUX POIRES
Watercress and Pear Salad

Watercress and sweet pear slices tossed in a light vinaigrette make a splendid warm-weather salad.

SERVES 4

1 small egg
½ teaspoon Dijon-style mustard
1 teaspoon finely chopped shallots
2 tablespoons cider vinegar
½ cup peanut, sunflower, or walnut oil

Salt and pepper
4 cups watercress, washed, with stems removed
¼ cup bread croutons
2 small ripe Anjou pears, peeled, halved, cored, and cut into thin slices.

1. In a bowl beat the egg for about 1 minute. Add the mustard, shallots, and cider vinegar. Mix well. Gradually drizzle in the oil, whisking vigorously until it thickens to the consistency of heavy cream. Season to taste.

2. In a large bowl add the watercress, croutons, and pear slices. Add the dressing and toss.

SALADE MÉLANGÉ
Mixed Salad

With half a wheel of Camembert cheese and a fresh loaf of Pain Brié (page 273), this salad would make the perfect ending to a meal.

SERVES 6 TO 8

2 medium beets
¼ cup cider vinegar
1 teaspoon Dijon-style
    mustard
¾ cup heavy cream
Salt and pepper
2 cups Boston or Bibb
    lettuce, trimmed,
    washed, and dried
2 cups chicory, trimmed,
    washed, and dried
1 cup Belgian endive,
    trimmed, washed, and
    dried
1 cup mâche or watercress,
    trimmed, washed, and
    dried
1 large apple (Granny
    Smith, Golden
    Delicious, or
    McIntosh), peeled,
    cored, halved, and
    thinly sliced
2 tablespoons chopped
walnuts

1. In a large pot bring the beets to a boil in enough water to cover and simmer for 2 hours. Remove from the heat and let them cool in their own water. When cool, trim the leaves and cut the beets into thin slices.

2. In a small bowl combine the cider vinegar and the mustard. Gradually whisk in the heavy cream until it thickens slightly. Season to taste.

3. In a serving bowl place the Boston lettuce, chicory, Belgian endive, mâche or watercress, apples, and beets. Pour the dressing over all and toss. Sprinkle the walnuts on top.

Desserts

*M*any people feel that Norman desserts are the perfect showcase for the region's chief culinary treasures: cream, butter, and apples. Since my first cooking attempt at the age of eight yielded crêpes filled with sugar, apples, and whipped cream, I understand the attraction of, although do not necessarily subscribe to, that line of thinking. In any case, there can be no question that Norman cooks and bakers have fulfilled the promise of this rich legacy with dozens of masterly confections. Tart Reinette and Calville apples are often included in such classic dessert recipes as the Carré Normand, rectangles of buttery puff pastry topped with apple slices; Bourdelots, baked apples filled with butter, sugar, and almonds and napped with a velvety cider mousse; and Crepiau, savory apple pancakes. Pears, peaches, and strawberries are also popular in Norman dessert recipes, particularly when baked in sweet tarts or flans or simply marinated in such brandies as Calvados and poiré.

A number of the more famous desserts are often a showcase for the talents of the bakers of a particular city or town. For instance, the pâtisseries of Cherbourg are proud to display their croustillons—small crispy cookies—while Avranches and the area around Mont-Saint-Michel boast of their sablés—light sugar cookies that have become a favorite of children throughout the Bocage. The city of Rouen is credited with having created two famous sweets—roulettes, individual coffee cakes rolled and folded similarly to puff pastry dough, and mirlitons, delicate almond tartlets. However, Rouen must share the credit for the mirlitons with the town of Pont-Audemer, which also lays claims to them.

In this chapter I have also included a Norman bread recipe, called pain brié, which my mother has been making for as long as I can recall and which was just too good to be left out of the book.

BEAU TÉNÈBREUX
Light Sponge Cake Filled with Whipped Cream Flavored with Calvados

A favorite Norman dessert. If raspberries or blueberries are in season, you may wish to cut back on the amount of chopped cake included in the filling and substitute the berries instead.

½ cup plus 2 tablespoons
   sugar
4 egg yolks

4 tablespoons cornstarch
2 tablespoons flour
4 egg whites

SERVES 8 TO 10

Filling
1 cup heavy cream
¼ cup sugar

1 teaspoon Calvados

Confectioners' sugar

1. Beat the sugar and the egg yolks together until light and lemon-colored. Stir in the cornstarch and flour.
2. Beat the egg whites to a stiff peak and fold them into the mixture.
3. Lightly butter and flour a round 10-inch cake pan 2 inches high. Pour in the mixture and bake in a preheated 325°F oven for 40 minutes. Cool in the pan for 5 minutes on a rack before turning out. Then unmold the cake onto a rack to cool.
4. When the cake has cooled, slice approximately ¼ inch off the top with a long, sharp knife and set aside.
5. Then make a wide, shallow well in the center by cutting out a ¾-inch-deep by 8-inch-wide circle of cake. Don't worry about removing the circle in a single piece—it gets chopped up later.
6. To make the filling, whip the heavy cream, sugar, and Calvados together to a soft peak. Dice the circle of cake into small pieces and fold into the whipped cream. Spoon this mixture into the well. If you are using fresh fruit, discard the unused cake.
7. Replace the top of the cake, sprinkle with confectioners' sugar, and serve.

BÛCHE DE NOËL
Rolled Christmas Cake

This holiday cake is as much a tradition in Normandy as the hanging of the sabots, or wooden shoes, over the fireplace on Christmas Eve. Since Bûche de Noël literally means Yule log, the idea is to decorate the cake to look as much like a log as possible. For a little extra zest, you may wish to add a tablespoon or two of Calvados or Benedictine to the sugar syrup.

SERVES 10

Cake Batter
5 tablespoons butter
4 whole eggs
½ cup sugar

¼ cup plus 2 tablespoons flour
2 tablespoons cornstarch

Buttercream Filling
½ cup sugar
3 eggs, lightly beaten
3 sticks butter at room temperature

2 ounces semisweet chocolate

Syrup
¼ cup sugar
Calvados or Benedictine, to taste (optional)

Confectioners' sugar (optional)

1. To prepare the cake batter, heat the butter in a small saucepan until just melted. Keep warm.
2. Separate the eggs, reserving both the yolks and the whites.
3. In a medium bowl, combine the yolks with the sugar and whip until they are lemony in color, about 5 minutes.
4. In a large bowl, whip the whites to soft peaks. Fold the yolks and sugar mixture gently into the whites.
5. Combine the flour and cornstarch and gently fold into the egg mixture. Gently fold in the melted butter; the batter should remain as fluffy as possible.

6. Butter a 10-inch by 15-inch jelly roll pan. Cut a piece of wax paper to fit the pan and press along the bottom.

7. Pour the batter gently over the paper and spread evenly with a spatula; it should only be about ¼-inch deep.

8. Place the pan in a preheated 400° oven for 12 to 15 minutes, or until the dough springs back when pressed with your fingers. Do not overcook, or the cake will dry out.

9. Cool the cake in its pan for 5 minutes on a wire rack before removing from the pan. The wax paper should adhere to the bottom of the cake. Let it cool.

10. While the cake is cooling, prepare the buttercream filling. In a small pot combine the sugar with ¼ cup water and cook to the thread stage, about 230°F to 235°F on a candy thermometer. You can also test the sugar by dropping a little into a bowl of cold water. Pinch the sugar between your thumb and forefinger, and then slowly open your fingers. If the sugar forms a thread, it is ready.

11. In a large bowl, pour the sugar mixture over the eggs and whip rapidly and vigorously until nearly cool and fluffy.

12. Add the softened butter about 2 tablespoons at a time and continue to mix well. Reserve buttercream at room temperature until needed.

13. To prepare the syrup, in a small pot combine the sugar with ¼ cup water. Bring to a boil, remove from the heat, and cool. If you wish, add the Calvados or Benedictine to taste at this point.

14. Remove the wax paper gently from the cake, and with a sharp knife, trim the edges of cake until even. Brush the cake with the sugar syrup, allowing the syrup to completely soak in. Then spread half of the buttercream mixture over the cake with a spatula.

15. Starting at one of the short sides of the cake, gently roll the cake away from you into a cylinder.

16. Take ½ tablespoon of the buttercream and make a small mound the size of half a walnut shell on top of the roll. Repeat the process three more times, placing the small mounds of buttercream at varying points along the top of the roll; these are meant to represent "knots" in the wood. Reserve the remaining buttercream. Refrigerate the roll for 1 hour.

17. About 10 minutes before you remove the roll from the refrigerator, melt the semisweet chocolate in a double boiler. Combine the melted chocolate with the remaining buttercream.

18. Remove the cake from the refrigerator and cover all sides evenly with the chocolate buttercream. Transfer to a serving plate, and place the cake in the refrigerator for 30 minutes more.

19. Remove the cake from the refrigerator and with a small, sharp knife, cut a small section off the tops of each of the "knots"—just enough to let the white buttercream show through.

20. With a fork, score the surface of the chocolate lengthwise to resemble wood bark. Dip the fork in hot water occasionally to facilitate this process.

21. Refrigerate the cake for at least 1 hour before serving. Sprinkle the Bûche de Noël with confectioners' sugar and serve cold.

CARRÉ NORMAND
Norman Square

Flaky puff pastry topped with sliced apples and crème fraîche makes an elegant Norman dessert. This is a relatively simple version, but if you choose, you may substitute about ¼ cup honey and the juice of ¼ lemon for the sugar. Mix it together and warm it slightly in a pan so it becomes easier to brush onto the sliced apples. Sprinkle a little Calvados on top of the tart just before you place it in the oven if you like. Pears, peaches, or plums are also good fruits for toppings.

6 apples (Granny Smith or
    McIntosh), peeled and
    cored
¼ lemon
16 ounces Puff Pastry
    Dough (page 24;
    approximately ⅓
    recipe; or purchase
    frozen)

Sugar
1 cup Crème Fraîche (page
    23) or ¼ cup heavy
    cream, whipped

SERVES 6

1. Rub the peeled and cored apples with the lemon, then set
aside.
2. On a floured board or table, roll out the puff pastry dough
into a 12- by 12-inch square. Place the square on a buttered
baking sheet.
3. Cut each apple in half, then cut in ¼-inch slices.
4. Starting at the top of the dough square, make one row of
apples across. Then make a second row, overlapping the first
row of apples by approximately ⅓. Continue until the square
is completely covered with apple slices.
5. Sprinkle the apples with sugar and bake the tart in a preheated 450°F oven for 20 minutes. Serve immediately with
crème fraîche or whipped cream.

CHAUSSONS AUX POMMES
Apple Turnovers

MAKES 4 TURNOVERS

2 tablespoons butter
4 medium apples (Granny Smith, Golden Delicious, or McIntosh), peeled, cored, and diced
¼ cup plus 1 tablespoon sugar

Pinch of cinnamon
12 ounces Puff Pastry Dough (page 24, approximately ¼ recipe; or purchase frozen)
1 egg yolk

1. Melt the butter in a skillet. Add the diced apples and sauté over medium heat for 4 to 5 minutes, or until they begin to brown. Add ¼ cup of the sugar and the cinnamon and stir well. Remove from the heat, place the mixture on a plate, and cool in the refrigerator.

2. Meanwhile, divide the puff pastry dough into 4 equal pieces, approximately 3 ounces each. On a lightly floured board or table, roll out the dough into circles approximately ⅛ inch thick by 8 inches in diameter. You may want to use an 8-inch plate as a template: simply set it on the pastry circles and cut around it with a small, sharp knife.

3. Remove the apple mixture from the refrigerator when cool and divide into quarters, placing some on ½ of each pastry circle.

4. Mix the egg yolk with 1 tablespoon water and brush a little around the edge of each pastry. Fold in half and seal the edges by gently pressing with your fingertips and then with the tines of a fork. Brush the dough with the rest of the egg and water mixture, and sprinkle each turnover with the remaining sugar.

5. Place on a baking pan in a preheated 450°F oven for 15 minutes, or until browned. Remove from the oven, cool, and serve.

LA FALLUE
Norman Coffee Cake

This sweet raised cake is a favorite breakfast treat, but we usually ate it for dessert with fresh Terrinée (page 266) and strong coffee laced with my father's Calvados.

1 package active dry yeast
or 1 tablespoon
granulated yeast
3¾ cups flour
2 teaspoons salt

4 tablespoons sugar
⅓ cup Crème Fraîche (page 23)
5 eggs
6 tablespoons butter

SERVES 8 TO 10

1. In a large bowl dissolve the yeast in 3 tablespoons lukewarm water.
2. Add the flour, salt, sugar, crème fraîche, and 4 eggs. Knead the dough until smooth.
3. Gradually work the butter into the dough a small piece at a time. After all of the butter has been incorporated, knead the dough for 3 to 4 minutes.
4. Put the dough back into the bowl, cover with a clean cloth, and let it rise for 3 hours at room temperature, or until at least double in size.
5. Punch the dough down and refrigerate for 2 hours.
6. Remove the dough from the refrigerator and cut in half. Shape both halves into ovals and place on a baking sheet or large bread molds. Let the cakes rise for 1 hour and 30 minutes at room temperature.
7. Brush each cake with a wash made from 1 egg and 1 tablespoon water. Then, with a small, sharp knife, make 3 lengthwise cuts, about ⅛ inch deep, along the top of each cake.
8. Bake the cakes in a preheated 375°F oven for 45 to 50 minutes, or until lightly browned. Remove from the pans and let cool on a rack. Slice and serve warm.

GALETTE DE L'AVRANCHIN
Sweet Layered Tart

The galette is known throughout France as Twelfth Night Cake and is traditionally eaten on January 6 in various forms and with numerous fillings. However, this version from Avranches differs in that the pastry is crisper and rises less than in the more festive galettes. Apples are arranged on the top layer, but you can use any fruit available.

SERVES 8 TO 10

Pastry
2 cups flour
12 tablespoons butter
¾ cup sugar
½ teaspoon vanilla extract

½ teaspoon baking powder
3 egg yolks
1 whole egg

4 Golden Delicious apples,
   peeled, cored, and cut
   into 8 segments each

2 tablespoons butter

Pastry Cream
2 cups milk
1 vanilla bean
4 egg yolks

½ cup sugar
4 tablespoons cornstarch or
   potato starch

1 teaspoon confectioners'
   sugar

1. To make the pastry, place the flour in a large bowl and add the butter in small pieces. Mix well by hand or with an electric mixer. Add the sugar and continue to mix until the dough takes on a sandy consistency.
2. Add the vanilla extract, baking powder, egg yolks, and whole egg and continue to mix. Form the dough into a ball and refrigerate for at least 1 hour.
3. Divide the dough into 3 equal parts, and on a lightly floured board or table, roll out the dough into circles that are 10 inches

in diameter and approximately ¼ inch thick. Trim any excess so the circles are approximately equal.

4. Place on lightly buttered baking sheets and bake in a pre-heated 350°F oven for 30 to 40 minutes, or until lightly browned. Remove gently and cool.

5. While the pastry is baking, brown the apple segments. Melt the butter in a skillet. Add the apples and sauté on both sides over low-to-medium heat. Set aside.

6. To make the pastry cream, in a saucepan bring the milk and vanilla bean to a boil. Reduce the heat and simmer for 2 or 3 minutes.

7. In a bowl mix the egg yolks and the sugar until they are lemon-colored. Add the cornstarch and mix well.

8. Remove the vanilla bean from the milk and reserve. Gradually pour the hot milk into the egg-and-sugar mixture, stirring constantly. Then transfer everything back into the saucepan. Stir constantly over medium heat until the mixture begins to thicken. As soon as 2 or 3 bubbles rise to the surface, remove the saucepan from the heat.

9. Spread the pastry cream evenly on the pastry circles to within a ¼ inch of the edge. Stack the circles on top of each other. On the top layer, arrange the apple segments and sprinkle with confectioners' sugar.

GÂTEAU AU BEURRE
Butter Cake

A light, buttery cake that is excellent served with fresh raspberries or strawberries and a little crème fraîche.

¾ cup plus 2 tablespoons sugar	16 tablespoons butter, melted	SERVES 6
Pinch of salt	1¼ cups flour	
4 large eggs, separated		

1. In a bowl beat together the sugar, salt, and egg yolks until lemon-colored.

2. Gradually stir in the melted butter.

3. Sift the flour into the mixture, then fold in gently.

4. In a separate bowl beat the egg whites to a soft peak. Fold the whites into the batter ⅓ at a time. Do not overwork.

5. Lightly butter and flour an 8- by 8- by 2-inch mold. Pour the batter into the mold and place in a preheated 350°F oven for 25 minutes. During that time the cake should pull away from the sides slightly.

6. Cool in the mold for 5 minutes on a rack before turning out. Unmold the cake onto a rack and cool to room temperature before serving.

LES ROULETTES
Rolled Flaky Coffee Cakes

The rolling and folding process called for in this preparation is very similar to that for Puff Pastry Dough (page 24). Serve these light rich cakes for breakfast, lunch, or dessert.

MAKES 18
CAKES

1¼ cups milk
1 package active dry yeast
  or 1 tablespoon
  granulated yeast
3½ cups flour
2 teaspoons salt
2 tablespoons sugar

4 tablespoons butter,
  melted
12 tablespoons butter
2 egg yolks

1. In a saucepan heat the milk until lukewarm (about 90°F). Pour into a large bowl, add the yeast, and dissolve well.

2. Add the flour, salt, sugar, and melted butter and mix for 2 to 3 minutes; the dough should have a sticky consistency. Let it rise at room temperature for 1 hour and 30 minutes, or until double in size. Punch it down, cover, and refrigerate for 3 hours.

3. In a chilled bowl by hand knead the 12 tablespoons butter until soft and pliable.

4. Remove the dough from the refrigerator and place on a lightly floured board or table. Flour the dough slightly and roll out into a rectangle that is approximately 18 inches long by 12 inches wide by ⅛ inch thick.

5. Take the kneaded butter and spread it over the bottom ⅔ of the rectangle to within ½ inch of the edge. Then fold the top ⅓ of the rectangle down over the center, and fold the bottom ⅓ over that. Refrigerate for 30 minutes.

6. Remove the dough from the refrigerator and return to the floured board or table, with the seam to the left. Roll out to the same dimensions and repeat the folding procedure. Refrigerate for 20 minutes.

7. Repeat rolling and folding procedure another time and refrigerate for 1 hour.

8. Remove the dough from the refrigerator, and again on a lightly floured board or table, place the dough with the seam to the left. Gently roll out to the same dimensions. Then, with a sharp knife, cut 18 3- by 4-inch rectangles. Roll them into 3-inch-wide cylinders and place them on buttered cookie sheets with a few inches between each. Cover the cylinders with clean towels or plastic wrap and let them rise at room temperature for 2 hours.

9. Lightly beat the 2 egg yolks with 2 tablespoons lukewarm water and brush over the cakes.

10. Bake in a preheated 450°F oven for 8 to 10 minutes, or until lightly browned. Cool and serve.

SAINT EVE
A Sweet Meringue

Credit for this recipe must be given to a small patisserie owned by P. Dupont in the city of Bayeaux. The shop's specialty is a delicate meringue pastry called Saint Eve which I was fortunate enough to taste the last time I was in Normandy. Unfortunately, I was in a rush and wasn't able to ask for the recipe.

Rather than omitting it from the book altogether, however, I experimented with a few meringues and buttercream fillings until I had approximated the original. The following version is close, if not precisely the Saint Eve itself. For a variation top with whipped cream and fresh fruit, and dust with confectioner's sugar.

SERVES 6

Meringues

¼ cup hazelnuts or almonds, crushed or ground

5 egg whites
1 cup plus 2 tablespoons sugar

Buttercream Filling

¼ cup sugar
2 small eggs, lightly beaten

12 tablespoons butter, room temperature

1. To prepare the meringue spread the hazelnuts or almonds on a sheet pan and bake in a preheated 350°F oven until lightly browned. Remove and cool.

2. In a large bowl whip the egg whites to stiff peaks. Gently fold in the sugar and nuts; avoid overfolding the mixture.

3. Place the mixture in a pastry bag fitted with either a ½-inch nozzle or no nozzle at all. Gently pipe the mixture out onto a greased cookie sheet, making 12 circles approximately 4 inches in diameter by ½ inch high.

4. Bake the meringues in a preheated 200°F oven for 40 minutes. Remove from the oven and let cool.

5. While the meringues are cooling, prepare the buttercream filling. In a small pot combine the sugar with ⅛ cup of water and cook to the thread stage—about 230°F to 235°F on a candy thermometer. You can also test the sugar by dropping a little into a bowl of cold water. Pinch the sugar between your thumb and forefinger, and then slowly open your fingers. If the sugar forms a thread, it is ready.

6. In a medium bowl pour the sugar mixture over the eggs and whip rapidly and vigorously until nearly cool and fluffy.

7. Add the softened butter about 2 tablespoons at a time and continue to mix well. Reserve buttercream at room temperature until needed.

8. When the meringues have cooled, spread 2 to 3 tablespoons of buttercream on the bottom surface of each one. Place another shell bottom down on the buttercream filling, making it into a sandwich.

9. Repeat step 8 five more times.

These desserts can be kept up to 1 week in an airtight container.   NOTE

PÂTE SUCRÉE
Sugar Dough for Tarts

1½ cups flour
8 tablespoons butter,
    chilled
½ cup sugar

½ teaspoon vanilla extract   MAKES 1 PIE
¼ teaspoon baking powder   SHELL
1 egg, slightly beaten

1. In a food processor fitted with a plastic blade or by hand, mix the flour, butter, and sugar until crumbly.

2. Add the vanilla extract, baking powder, and egg. Continue to mix until the dough binds; in a food processor, this should take only 10 to 15 seconds.

3. Seal the dough in plastic wrap and refrigerate for 2 hours before using.

MIRLITONS DE PONT-AUDEMER
Almond Tartlets

This recipe is a Norman classic from the picturesque town of Pont-Audemer. The city of Rouen boasts a similar tart recipe. Serve warm with coffee for dessert or as a snack.

MAKES 4 TARTLETS

1 recipe Pâte Sucrée (page 249)
1 egg
¼ cup sugar

2 tablespoons ground almonds
1 tablespoon heavy cream

1. On a lightly floured board or table, roll out the pâte sucrée about ⅛ inch thick. Fit the dough into 4 small buttered molds approximately 3 inches in diameter by ½ inch high. Set aside.
2. In a saucepan over low heat beat the egg and the sugar together for 3 to 4 minutes, or until thick and fluffy. Fold in the ground almonds and the heavy cream.
3. Divide the mixture among the 4 molds and bake in a preheated 350°F oven for 20 minutes, or until lightly browned. Cool in the molds for 5 minutes on a rack before turning out. Unmold and cool on a rack.

TARTE AU FROMAGE BLANC
Cheese Tart

A simple traditional dessert.

SERVES 6 TO 8

1 recipe Pâte Sucrée (page 249)
1½ cups Fromage Blanc (page 270), at room temperature

¼ cup sugar
½ teaspoon grated lemon zest
3 eggs

1. On a lightly floured board or table, roll out the pâte sucrée about ⅛ inch thick. Fit it into a 10-inch tart pan with a remov-

able bottom. Wrap the remaining dough in waxed paper and refrigerate.

2. Line the inside of the tart pastry shell with aluminum foil and bake in a preheated 350°F for 15 minutes, just long enough to cook the shell halfway. Remove from the oven and carefully peel away the foil.

3. While the tart shell is baking, mix together the fromage blanc, sugar, and grated lemon peel. Stir in the egg one at a time and continue to stir for 3 or 4 minutes.

4. Pour the cheese mixture into the partially baked tart shell.

5. Lower the oven temperature to 300°F and bake the tart for 40 to 45 minutes, or until a knife inserted in the center comes out clean. Remove from the oven and cool on a rack. Serve at room temperature.

TARTE À LA RHUBARBE
Rhubarb Tart

Rhubarb was introduced into Normandy sometime during the late Middle Ages; it was originally cultivated by monks for medicinal purposes. The leaves of the plant are never eaten, only the stems, which are used in rich jams and tarts.

SERVES 8 TO 10

*Pâte à Tarte in Flan de
   Moules Caennaise
   (page 55)*
*4 cups rhubarb, outer skin
   removed, cut into
   ¼-inch pieces*
*¼ cup plus 2 tablespoons
   sugar*

2 eggs
½ cup heavy cream
*2 tablespoons butter,
   melted*
Pinch of cinnamon

1. On a lightly floured board or table, roll out the pâte à tarte ⅛ inch thick. Place it in a 10-inch quiche or tart pan with a removable bottom. Press the dough in until it conforms to the pan. Trim the excess dough—there should be enough for another tart shell—and reserve sealed in plastic wrap in the re-

frigerator. Let the molded dough rest in the refrigerator for 15 minutes before filling.

2. Arrange the diced rhubarb in the bottom of the tart shell and sprinkle with the sugar. Place the tart in a preheated 350°F oven for 20 minutes.

3. While the tart is baking, mix together the eggs, heavy cream, melted butter, and cinnamon. After 20 minutes, pour the custard mixture into the tart and return to the oven for 25 minutes, or until the custard has cooked. Cool and serve at room temperature.

NOTE   *Using the same recipe, you can also make an apple tart. Simply substitute 5 Granny Smith apples, peeled, cored, and cut into 8 pieces each, for the rhubarb.*

BOURDELOTS
Stuffed Baked Apples in Pastry

Normans love fruit baked in pastry, and Bourdelots is one of the classic recipes of the province. A similar preparation, Les Douillons Rouennais, includes pears instead of apples, but for all practical purposes, the recipes are the same. Peaches or plums may also be used.

1 cup plus 2 tablespoons sugar
1 clove
4 Golden Delicious apples, peeled and cored
12 ounces Puff Pastry Dough (page 24, approximately ¼ recipe; or purchase frozen) or 1 recipe Pâte à Tarte in Flan de Moules Caennaise (page 55)

2 tablespoons ground almonds
1 tablespoon butter
2 egg yolks

MAKES 4

Cider Mousse
2 egg yolks
¼ cup sugar

¼ cup cider

1. In a large saucepan bring 2 cups water, 1 cup of the sugar, and the clove to a boil. Place the apples in the water 2 at a time and simmer for 4 to 5 minutes. Remove the apples from the syrup with a slotted spoon and cool.
2. On a lightly floured board or table, roll out the puff pastry dough into a 12-inch square, approximately ⅛ inch thick. With a knife cut into 4 6-inch squares. Set aside.
3. To make the filling, in a bowl cream the remaining 2 tablespoons sugar, ground almonds, butter, and 1 egg yolk.
4. Turn the poached apples stem side down and place 1 in the center of each dough square. Divide the filling equally among the apples and place in the core. Bring the dough up around

the apples, pinching the edges together with your fingertips and trimming the excess dough with a small knife.

5. Turn the apples over and place them on a lightly buttered cookie sheet or baking pan. Brush the dough with a mixture of 1 egg yolk and 1 tablespoon water.

6. Bake in a preheated 450°F oven for 15 to 20 minutes, or until lightly browned.

7. While the apples are baking, make the cider mousse. In a saucepan over low heat, whip together the egg yolks, sugar, and cider by hand until fluffy and thick; this should take 6 to 7 minutes. Cool.

8. Remove the apples from the oven and cool at room temperature for 10 minutes. Spoon the cider mousse over each apple and serve.

LES BONTONS
Vanilla Cookies

These light cookies are favorites among the children in the province, and my mother used to bake them as treats for us.

2 DOZEN COOKIES

4 tablespoons plus approximately 1 teaspoon butter
5 tablespoons sugar
6 tablespoons flour
1 egg white
1¼ teaspoons vanilla extract

1. In a bowl cream 4 tablespoons of the butter and the sugar together. Add the flour and mix well.

2. Stir in the egg white and the vanilla extract.

3. With the remaining teaspoon butter grease the cookie sheets. If you have a pastry bag with a small nozzle, pipe out approximately 2 dozen cookies on the cookie sheet. Use about 1 tablespoon of batter for each cookie and space the cookies about 1 inch apart. If you do not have a pastry bag, use a tablespoon instead.

4. Bake the cookies in a preheated 400°F oven for 7 to 8 minutes, or until lightly browned. Remove from the oven, cool on a rack, and store in an airtight container.

CROUSTILLONS
Crispy Norman Cookies

Pale brown on the outside and white on the inside, crispy Croustillons are wonderful as accompaniments for mousse or fresh fruits.

⅓ cup sugar	¾ cup flour	3 DOZEN
3 tablespoons butter	½ teaspoon baking powder	COOKIES
1 tablespoon milk	2 egg whites	

1. In a small bowl mix the sugar, butter, and milk until creamy.
2. Add the flour, baking powder, and egg whites and continue to mix until smooth.
3. Spoon the mixture onto lightly buttered cookie sheets. Use about 1 tablespoon of batter for each cookie and space the cookies 1 inch apart.
4. Bake in a preheated 375°F oven for 12 minutes, or until lightly browned. Remove from the oven, cool on a rack, and store in an airtight container.

SABLÉS
Norman Sugar Cookies

A classic sugar cookie found throughout the province, although occasionally under such names as galette or petit beurre. Serve as an accompaniment to other desserts, particularly those with apples.

1 DOZEN
COOKIES

2 cups flour
8 tablespoons butter
½ cup sugar
5 egg yolks

Pinch of salt
1 teaspoon vanilla extract
2 tablespoons milk

1. Place the flour in a large bowl and add the butter in small pieces. Mix well by hand or with an electric mixer. Add the sugar and continue to mix until the dough takes on a sandy consistency.

2. Add 4 of the egg yolks, the salt, and vanilla extract and continue to mix. Form the dough into a ball, seal in plastic wrap and refrigerate for at least 1 hour.

3. Remove the dough from the refrigerator and roll out into a sheet approximately ¼ inch thick. With a cookie cutter or a knife, cut the dough into 2-inch circles. Place on lightly buttered cookie sheets.

4. Mix the remaining egg yolk with the milk. Brush a small amount on each cookie. Then, with the tip of a small knife, make 6 or 7 stripes on top of each cookie.

5. Bake in a preheated 350°F for 15 minutes, or until lightly browned. Remove from the oven, cool on a rack, and store in an airtight container.

FRAISES MARINÉES
AUX CALVADOS
Strawberries Marinated in Calvados

The farmer down the road from us grew one field of strawberries every year, and on particularly warm days, my brothers and sisters and I would creep in and help ourselves. He caught us once or twice but never really seemed to mind.

4 cups fresh strawberries
(use smaller
strawberries so you do
not have to cut them),
washed and dried,
with stems removed

2 tablespoons Calvados
¼ cup sugar
1 cup heavy cream
Cinnamon

SERVES 4

1. Place the strawberries in a bowl and add the Calvados. Let them marinate for at least 1 hour.
2. Add the sugar, mix gently, and set aside.
3. Whip the heavy cream to a stiff peak. Place a bed of whipped cream on each plate, leaving a slight hollow in the center for the strawberries. Lightly sprinkle the cinnamon around the edge of the cream. Place the strawberries in the center. Serve with Sablés (page 255).

PÊCHES DU NORMANDE
Peaches, Norman Style

An elegant preparation for fresh peaches.

4 fresh peaches, ripe but
firm
2 tablespoons butter
¼ cup sugar

Pinch of cinnamon
Pinch of ground cloves
1 tablespoon Calvados
½ cup heavy cream

SERVES 4

1. Place the peaches in a saucepan with enough water to cover. Bring to a boil and simmer for 1 minute. Drain in a colander and cool the peaches under cold running water. When they have cooled, peel and halve them, and remove the pits.
2. In a medium skillet melt the butter. Sprinkle the sugar into the butter. Place the peaches on the sugar, curved surface down. Cook for approximately 5 minutes over low heat.
3. Turn the peaches over, flat side down, and continue to cook

for another 5 minutes. The sugar will begin to brown lightly
and the peaches should become tender.

4. Add the cinnamon, ground cloves, Calvados, and the heavy
cream to the skillet. Simmer for 10 minutes more.

5. Arrange the peach halves on a platter or individual plates
and pour the sauce over them.

GOURMANDISE DOMFRONTAISE
Fresh Pears Baked
with Pear Brandy and Cream

The town of Domfront in Lower Normandy is famous for its
pears and pale pear brandy, poiré. You may serve this dish hot
out of the oven or warm.

SERVES 4

4 Anjou pears, peeled,
*   halved, and cored*
1 tablespoon poiré or pear
*   brandy*
¼ cup plus 1 tablespoon
*   sugar*

3 eggs
Pinch of salt
Pinch of cinnamon
½ cup heavy cream
1 tablespoon flour

1. Cut each pear into 8 sections. Arrange them in the bottom
of a large casserole, earthenware dish, or baking pan.

2. Sprinkle with poiré and 1 tablespoon of the sugar. Place in
a preheated 350°F oven for 15 to 20 minutes.

3. Meanwhile, mix together ¼ cup sugar and the eggs until
they are lemon-colored. Then stir in the salt, cinnamon, heavy
cream, and flour.

4. Pour the mixture over the pears and continue to bake for
35 to 40 minutes, or until lightly browned.

POMMES AU FOUR AU PAYSANNE
Baked Apples with Cider and Butter

These apples make a wonderful warm dessert for a chilly fall evening. You may even want to sprinkle them with a little Calvados while still in the oven.

6 *Golden Delicious apples*   *2 tablespoons sugar*   SERVES 6
2 tablespoons butter   *1 cup cider*

1. Core the apples, leaving the skin on. Then, with a small, sharp knife, make an incision completely around the apple about ¾ of the way from the bottom and ⅛ inch deep. Place the apples in a small casserole or ovenproof dish.
2. Cream the butter and sugar and divide the mixture among the 6 apples, placing a little in each.
3. Pour the cider around the apples. Bake in a preheated 350° F oven for 45 to 60 minutes, or until the apples are tender. Serve warm with a little cider spooned over them.

BEIGNETS DE POMMES
Apple Fritters

The fritter batter used in this recipe is quite simple and very Norman. For a richer-tasting batter, substitute good beer for the water—not really particularly Norman, but very tasty. Serve these as an accompaniment for veal and pork dishes, for dessert, or as a snack sprinkled with confectioners' sugar and cinnamon, and served with Crème aux Oeufs (page 271).

4 *apples (Granny Smith or*   SERVES 4
   McIntosh), peeled and   *2 eggs*
   cored   *Pinch of salt*
1 *tablespoon sugar*   ¼ *teaspoon baking powder*
1½ *cups flour*   4 *cups peanut oil*

1. Slice the apples into ¼-inch-thick rings. Arrange them on a large plate, sprinkle with the sugar, and let rest for 30 minutes.
2. Meanwhile, make the batter. In a bowl, combine the flour, eggs, salt, baking powder, and ¾ cup warm water or beer. Beat by hand into a light smooth batter.
3. In a heavy pot bring the peanut oil to 350°F. You will need a heavy-duty thermometer to measure.
4. Dip each apple ring into the batter, then gently slip it into the hot oil. Let the ring swim for about 5 minutes, or until golden brown. Remove from the oil and drain on paper towels. Serve warm.

CHARLOTTE AUX POMMES
Warm Apple Charlotte

The apple charlotte is purported to be the first fruit charlotte made in France. In any case, it is certainly the most popular in Normandy. Some recipes recommend that it be served with an apricot sauce, but I have always preferred it with Crème aux Oeufs (page 271). To make this dish, you will need a charlotte mold approximately 6 inches across by 3 inches deep.

SERVES 6 TO 8

*12 to 15 slices Pain Brié
  (page 273) or same
  amount good white
  bread, cut into ¼-inch
  slices
6 tablespoons butter,
  melted*

*6 cups apples, peeled,
  cored, and cubed
¼ cup sugar
⅛ teaspoon cinnamon*

1. Cut the crusts from the bread. Lightly brush both sides of each slice with approximately 1 teaspoon of the melted butter.
2. Line the bottom of the mold with 3 to 4 slices of buttered bread cut in triangles; they should overlap by approximately ¼ inch. Then line the sides with 6 to 8 slices cut in rectangles that are the same height as the mold; they should also overlap. Set aside. Reserve 3 slices of bread for the topping.

3. Sauté the diced apples in the remaining butter for 3 to 4 minutes and add the sugar and cinnamon. Stir well and cook for 1 to 2 minutes more. Pour the apples into the bread-lined mold and press down lightly with the back of a spoon. Cover with the reserved slices of buttered bread cut to fit the space.
4. Place the mold on a sheet pan and bake in a preheated 350° F oven for 45 minutes. Cool for 30 minutes and unmold onto a serving platter.

CREPIAU
Apple Pancakes

A superb accompaniment for pork dishes, these pancakes may also be served for dessert or breakfast sprinkled with sugar and crème fraîche.

½ cup milk
Pinch of salt
1 tablespoon sugar
2 eggs
1 cup flour

1 Granny Smith apple,
*   peeled, cored, and*
*   grated*
2 tablespoons butter

SERVES 4

1. In a bowl combine the milk, salt, sugar, and eggs. Place the flour in another bowl, then gradually pour the milk and egg mixture over it, mixing until smooth.
2. Add the grated apple to the mixture.
3. Melt the butter in a skillet. When it has begun to foam, add about ¼ cup batter to the skillet and let it cook slowly on one side until almost firm. Flip the pancake and cook the other side. Remove from the pan and keep warm. Repeat the procedure until all the batter has been used.

SORBETS DE POMMES CALVADOS
Apple Sherbet with Calvados

This recipe can be prepared in an ice-cream machine or in your freezer. Either preparation will yield a rich, refreshing dessert. A number of other sherbet recipes I have seen require that egg whites be whipped in during the freezing process to keep the sherbet from freezing too solidly. However, I've found that the addition of pulped fruit—in this case, the apples —serves the same end.

SERVES 4 TO 6

1 cup sugar
Zest of 1 lemon
4 medium apples (Granny Smith or Golden Delicious), peeled, cored, and halved

1 tablespoon lemon juice
1 teaspoon Calvados

1. In a saucepan bring the sugar and 2 cups of water to a boil. Add the lemon zest, apples, and lemon juice. Simmer for 45 minutes over low heat, or until the apples are tender. Remove from the heat and cool the apples in the syrup completely.
2. When the mixture has cooled, purée in a blender or food processor. Add the Calvados.
3. If you are going to use an ice-cream machine, first chill the mixture in the refrigerator for 3 hours. Then pour it into the ice-cream machine and process for 30 to 40 minutes, or until creamy. Freeze until you are ready to serve.
4. If you are not using an ice-cream machine, place the mixture in the freezer. As soon as the mixture begins to freeze, remove it from the freezer and beat vigorously by hand for 1 minute. Return to the freezer and repeat the process 1 or 2 more times at 30-minute intervals. Keep frozen until ready to serve.

CRÊPES CALVADOS
Crêpes Filled with Sautéed Apples and Served with a Calvados-laced Sauce

Perhaps one of the finest ways to celebrate Normandy's most famous crop—the triumvirate of apples, cider, and Calvados blended into an elegant dessert.

SERVES 4
(8 CRÊPES)

Crêpes
½ recipe pancake batter in
La Ficelle Normande
(page 57)

Sauce
4 whole eggs
¼ cup sugar

½ cup cider
2 tablespoons Calvados

Filling
4 tablespoons butter
4 medium apples (Granny
Smith, Golden
Delicious, or
McIntosh), peeled,
cored, and diced

2 tablespoons sugar
1 tablespoon Calvados

1. Make the crêpes and set aside.
2. To make the sauce, in a double boiler or a small, heavy saucepan over low heat, whisk the eggs, sugar, cider, and Calvados. Continue to whisk gently for about 7 to 8 minutes, or until the mixture thickens and becomes frothy. Remove from the heat and keep warm.
3. To make the filling, melt the butter in a sauté pan. Add the apples and sauté over medium heat until golden brown; this should take about 4 to 5 minutes. Stir the sugar into the apples and butter. Add the Calvados and stir. Remove the mixture from the heat.
4. Divide the apple filling among the crêpes, then fold or roll them. Place on serving plates and spoon the warm sauce over them.

SALADE FRUITS AUX CIDRE DOUX
Fruit Salad with Sweet Apple Cider

A fresh and refreshing fruit salad. Since sugar has been added to the fruits to make them juicier, none has been added to the whipped cream. However, let your own taste determine whether to add a little.

SERVES 6

2 peaches
1 cup Granny Smith apple, peeled, cored, halved, and thinly sliced
1 cup strawberries, washed and halved, with stems removed
1 cup raspberries, washed

2 oranges, peeled and segmented
4 apricots, quartered and pitted
¼ cup sugar
1 cup sweet cider
½ cup heavy cream

1. In a saucepan place the peaches in enough boiling water to cover and simmer for 1 minute. Drain and cool under cold running water. Peel and halve them. Remove the pits, then cut into small segments.
2. Combine all the fruit in a large bowl, add the sugar, and toss. Marinate in the refrigerator for 30 minutes. Add the cider and continue to refrigerate for 1 hour.
3. Whip the cream to a stiff peak. Serve the fruit salad on individual plates with a little whipped cream.

FLAN DE LOUVIERS
Sweet Flan

SERVES 8

Pâte Sucrée (page 249)
4 eggs
2 tablespoons butter, melted
¼ cup flour

1 tablespoon cornstarch
½ teaspoon grated lemon peel
Pinch of salt
2 cups milk

1. On a lightly floured board or table, roll out the pâte sucrée ⅛ inch thick. Fit it into a 10-inch tart pan with a removable bottom. Seal the extra dough in plastic wrap and refrigerate for another use.

2. Line the inside of the tart shell with aluminum foil and bake in a preheated 350°F oven for 15 minutes, just long enough to cook the shell halfway. Remove from the oven and carefully peel away the foil.

3. While the tart shell is baking, combine the eggs, melted butter, flour, cornstarch, lemon peel, and salt and mix well.

4. In a saucepan bring the milk to a boil. Gradually pour it into the custard mixture, stirring constantly.

5. Pour the custard into the tart shell and return the pan to the 350°F oven for 45 minutes, or until the top is lightly browned. Lower the heat if the custard begins to rise too quickly. Cool on a wire rack.

SOUFFLÉ GLAÇÉ AU CALVADOS
Frozen Soufflé Flavored with Calvados and Hazelnut Paste

Allow yourself two days to make this elegant frozen soufflé. It should remain in the freezer overnight.

4 egg yolks
3 whole eggs
¾ cup sugar
2 cups heavy cream

1 tablespoon Calvados
2 tablespoons hazelnut paste

SERVES 4

1. In a double boiler or a stainless steel bowl, vigorously whisk the egg yolks, whole eggs, and sugar together over low heat until fluffy and just lukewarm to the touch.

2. Remove from the heat. With an electric mixer or by hand, continue to beat the eggs and sugar until they thicken and cool; this should take 6 to 8 minutes.

3. Separately, whip the cream to a light, soft peak.
4. Mix the Calvados and hazelnut paste together and fold into the egg mixture. Then gently fold the whipped cream into the eggs.
5. Tape a length of aluminum foil completely around a 20-ounce soufflé mold so the foil extends 2 inches above the rim. Pour the mixture into the mold; it should come to within 1 inch of the top of the foil. Place it in the freezer overnight. Slice and serve the next day.

TERRINÉE
Baked Rice Pudding

Although rice is not used to any great extent in Norman cookery, this pudding is a favorite throughout the province. Be sure to use *uncooked* rice.

SERVES 4 TO 6

5 cups milk
1 vanilla bean or 1
   teaspoon vanilla
   extract
½ cup uncooked rice,
   washed

¾ cup sugar
2 tablespoons butter
Pinch of cinnamon
¼ teaspoon salt

1. In a saucepan, bring the milk and the vanilla bean to a boil.
2. Add the rice, and simmer for 30 minutes, stirring often.
3. Remove the bean and add the sugar, butter, cinnamon, and salt. Simmer for 1 minute.
4. Pour the mixture into a baking dish. Bake in a preheated 375°F oven for 30 to 40 minutes. During that time the top should brown and a light crust should form. If it does not, place the dish under the broiler for 1 or 2 minutes. Serve with La Fallue (page 243).

CROÛTE PAIN PERDU
À LA CRÈME FOUETTÉE
French Toast with
Puréed Apples and Cream

In this country pain perdu is known as French toast. However, this Norman recipe is a somewhat more elaborate treatment of that old favorite. Use La Fallue in this dish, if you have any; if not, a good white bread will do.

4 tablespoons butter
6 apples (Granny Smith,
    Golden Delicious, or
    McIntosh), peeled,
    cored, and diced
4 tablespoons sugar
3 eggs

1 cup milk
Pinch of cinnamon
8 slices La Fallue (page
    243) or any good firm
    sandwich bread
½ cup heavy cream

SERVES 4

1. Melt 2 tablespoons of the butter in a skillet. Add the apples and sauté for 8 to 10 minutes, or until very tender. Add 2 tablespoons of the sugar and continue to cook until the apples begin to turn pulpy. Remove from the heat and mash into a coarse purée. Set aside and keep warm.
2. In a large bowl combine the eggs, milk, remaining sugar, and cinnamon. Add the bread slices and let them soak for 2 to 3 minutes.
3. Melt the remaining butter in a skillet. Toast the bread on both sides, then set aside.
4. Whip the heavy cream to a stiff peak.
5. Place the toast on a baking sheet. Spoon some apple purée over each slice and top with 1 tablespoon whipped cream. Place under a very hot broiler and quickley brown the cream. Serve hot with the remaining whipped cream.

L'OMELETTE SOUFFLÉE BÉNÉDICTINE
Sweet Omelette with Benedictine

A superb dessert omelette or late-night snack.

SERVES 1

3 eggs
2 tablespoons sugar
1 tablespoon butter
1 tablespoon Benedictine

⅛ teaspoon confectioners'
* sugar*
¼ cup Crème aux Oeufs
* (page 271)*

1. In a bowl beat the eggs until fluffy, about 1 minute. Stir in the sugar.
2. Melt the butter in a skillet or omelette pan over low heat. Add the egg-and-sugar mixture. Do not cook the omelette too quickly; the center should remain slightly loose.
3. While the omelette is cooling, warm the Benedictine in a small saucepan.
4. Fold the omelette in half and slide onto a plate. Sprinkle with the confectioners' sugar, then gently pour the Benedictine over the omelette. Serve with crème aux oeufs.

CRÉMETS
Rich Dessert Cheese

In the United States this delicate dessert cheese is known as Coeur à la Crème. I have seen a number of recipes that use pot cheese, but this recipe from the Auge Valley is fairly basic.

½ cup heavy cream
2 cups Crème Fraîche (page 23)

2 egg whites
Confectioners' sugar
Raspberries or strawberries

SERVES 4

1. Whip the heavy cream to a soft peak and fold into the crème fraîche.
2. Whip the egg whites until stiff.
3. Fold the egg whites into the cream mixture and place in a coeur à la crème or heart-shaped mold covered with cheese-cloth. If you do not have a mold, line a colander with cheese-cloth and place the mixture in that. Drain into a dish for 24 hours in your refrigerator.
4. To serve, unmold the crémets, slice, sprinkle with a little confectioners' sugar, and serve with fresh raspberries or straw-berries.

FROMAGE BLANC
White Pot Cheese

This is a very basic recipe for homemade cheese. You can serve it as an appetizer or in salads, or you can mix it with a little sugar and serve with fresh fruit for dessert. I have included it in the recipe for Tarte au Fromage Blanc (page 250), a delicious dessert tart.

MAKES 3 TO 4
CUPS

½ tablet rennet
8 cups milk, at room
temperature
(approximately 80°F)

¼ cup Crème Fraîche (page
23) or heavy cream

1. In a large bowl dissolve the rennet in 2 tablespoons lukewarm water.
2. Add the milk to the rennet and water. Cover with a clean towel and leave at room temperature for 12 hours.
3. Place the bowl over a saucepan of simmering water—the bottom of the bowl should not touch the water—and warm the milk to approximately 110°F, or just warm to the touch. The whey will begin to separate from the curd at that temperature and float to the surface. Skim out the whey and place on a clean towel or paper towels to drain. When the curds and whey have stopped separating, place the whey in a blender. Discard the curds.
4. Add the crème fraîche or heavy cream to the blender and purée for 2 minutes until smooth. Keep refrigerated.

CRÈME AUX OEUFS
Sweet Cream and Egg Sauce

Serve this rich sauce with fresh fruit or sweet omelettes.

1 cup milk	*5 egg yolks*	MAKES 3 TO 4
1 cup heavy cream	*½ cup sugar*	CUPS
½ teaspoon vanilla extract		
or 1 vanilla bean		

1. In a saucepan bring the milk, heavy cream, and vanilla extract to a boil. Reduce the heat and simmer for 4 to 5 minutes.
2. Meanwhile, beat the egg yolks and sugar until they turn lemon-colored.
3. Gradually stir approximately ½ the milk and cream mixture into the eggs.
4. Over low heat pour the mixture back into the saucepan. Simmer until the mixture begins to thicken, 4 to 5 minutes. Do not boil.
5. Remove from the heat and strain through a cheesecloth into a bowl. Cool and serve.

GELÉE DE POMMES
Apple Jelly

A staple of the kitchens of Lower Normandy. Every autumn my mother would make enough apple jelly to see us through until the following year, and for a day or two afterward, the kitchen was thick with the warm, sweet smell of apples. She liked to use Reinettes in the jelly, but if there were a few stray Clos Rogers or Tête de Brebis about, they were included as well. I used to be so partial to fresh apple jelly that I would often forego the bread or toast and simply eat spoonfuls of it for dessert or as a snack.

4 CUPS

3 pounds apples (McCombs, Baldwin, or McIntosh)
3 cups fresh unsweetened cider or water

2 pounds sugar
2 tablespoons pectin
Paraffin

1. Wash the apples and remove the stems and tails. Cut into 8 pieces each but do not core. Place the apples in a large pot with 3 cups cider or water and bring to a boil. Boil for 10 minutes, stirring occasionally.

2. While the apples are boiling, line a colander with 2 or 3 layers of wet cheesecloth and place over a large bowl. Once the apples have cooked, pour the apples and the liquid into the colander. Allow the apples to drain at room temperature into the bowl for at least 8 hours.

3. After the apples have drained, pour all the liquid—you should have approximately 4 cups—back into a large heavy-bottomed pot. Add the sugar and the pectin, and bring to a rolling boil. Boil for 3 minutes, stirring constantly.

4. Let jelly rest for a few minutes before removing the skin. Pour the jelly into sterilized jars. Cool for a few minutes and then pour hot melted paraffin over the surface of the jelly. Let the paraffin cool and harden before covering jars with metal lids.

PAIN BRIÉ
Norman Bread

This fragrant, finely textured Norman bread is easy to prepare and goes well with just about anything. Pain brié literally translates to "crushed bread," a name derived from the particular pounding method used in this preparation to render a smoother, moist texture. You will need to begin this recipe a day in advance because the sponge, or "starter," must rest overnight. Once baked, the bread will remain moist and fresh in your refrigerator for up to a week.

2 packages active dry yeast or 2 tablespoons of granulated yeast
4 cups bread flour; if not available, use all-purpose flour

3 teaspoons salt

MAKES 1
LOAF

1. To make the sponge or starter, in a large bowl dissolve the yeast in 1 cup lukewarm water. After a minute or two, add 1 cup flour and mix. Then add the second cup and knead by hand until smooth; the dough should be dry and not stick to your hands. Cover the bowl with a towel and let it rise at room temperature overnight.
2. The next day punch the dough down. Add ¾ cup lukewarm water, the salt, and the remaining flour, again 1 cup at a time. Work the dough in the bowl until dry, then remove and knead on a lightly floured board or table for 5 minutes. The dough will be very firm.
3. Once you have kneaded the dough, pound it heavily with a rolling pin to flatten it. Fold the dough and pound again until flat. Repeat this procedure 7 or 8 times. Let the dough rest for 10 minutes.
4. Form the dough into a ball and cover with a piece of plastic wrap to keep moist. Let it rise for 2 hours and 30 minutes at room temperature.

5. With a small sharp knife, make 5 parallel cuts, approximately ¼ inch deep, along the top of the loaf.

6. Place the loaf on a lightly buttered baking sheet and bake in a preheated 425°F oven for 40 minutes, or until browned.

NOTE   *If you plan to make more Pain Brié in a few days, reserve approximately 1 cup uncooked dough for a starter.*

PAIN DE HONFLEUR
Norman Whole Wheat Bread

A simple and delicious bread recipe from the port city of Honfleur.

2 packages active dry yeast or 2 tablespoons granulated yeast
2 tablespoons sugar
¼ cup honey
1 pound whole wheat flour, sifted

1 pound unbleached flour, sifted
1 cup milk, lukewarm
6 tablespoons butter, melted
2 tablespoons salt

MAKES 2 LOAVES

1. In a large bowl dissolve the yeast in 1 cup of lukewarm water.
2. Add the sugar and honey to the yeast and water.
3. Add both flours, the milk, the melted butter, and the salt. Mix well. Knead the dough for 10 to 15 minutes.
4. Place the dough in a bowl, cover with a towel, and let it rise undisturbed in a warm place for 45 to 60 minutes, or until it has doubled in size.
5. Punch down the dough. Knead again for 2 to 3 minutes. Cut in half, and shape into two round loaves. Cover both loaves with a clean towel and let rise for another 1 hour and 30 minutes, or until almost double in size.
6. Place the loaves on a large baking sheet and bake in a preheated 400°F oven for 45 minutes, or until lightly browned. Cool the loaves on a rack.

For a richer bread, replace the water and milk with an equal amount of buttermilk. This bread can remain frozen for up to 6 weeks.

NOTE

A Note
on Calvados

*N*ot too much is known about the early history of Calvados despite its enormous popularity in Normandy. A few experts credit its invention to one Gilles de Gouberville, a native of the Cotentin who, in 1553, is said to have distilled "sydre" for the first time to obtain "eau de vie." This is probably a bit of local promotion, however, and it's more likely that Norman peasants had been distilling a reasonable facsimile of Calvados as early as the reign of Charlemagne.

Authorities appear to be more in agreement with regard to the origin of the name. In 1588, Philip II of Spain sent his Invincible Armada against England, and during a storm one of the ships, *El Calvador,* ran aground on the Norman coast. Gradually, the area began to be known by the name of that hapless ship—or at least a skewed pronounciation of it—until eventually, France's Constitutional Assembly made the name official in the nineteenth century. Within time, the apple brandy produced in and around that area took the name, as well.

In 1941 the government of France finally decided to impose a variation of the appellation controllée laws on the distillation and marketing of Calvados. These laws, established during the nineteenth century, regulated the production and sale of wine and other brandies. For the first time Calvados was accorded the same official status that had earlier been achieved by France's other famous brandies, Cognac and Armagnac. According to these laws there are only two methods of producing Calvados: through a single distillation in a continuous still or a double distillation in a pot still. The former method, used in ten of the eleven Calvados-producing districts of Normandy, is designated by the term *appellation réglementée* on the label. The double-distillation method is used only in the Pays d'Auge and can be distinguished by the term *appellation Pays d'Auge contrôllée.*

Those connoisseurs whose palates are already inclined toward the elegant smoothness of Cognac and Armagnac tend to prefer Calvados from the Pays d'Auge for a depth of flavor that is apparent even in its youth. On the other hand, single-distillation Calvados tends to retain more of the apple flavor and bouquet throughout its life, a characteristic many others regard as the most important distinction of a fine Calvados.

My father grows about fifteen different varieties of cider apples—I've heard that there are eighty-three in Normandy—and sells most to a local producer who uses the single-distillation method. The apples are first washed, then pressed into a thick pulp from which all the juice is extracted. The juice is then allowed to ferment for up to a month before being transferred as cider to large copper-lined alembics in the distillery.

The powerful spirit that eventually emerges from the alembic is Calvados in its purest form, a clear liquid with an alcohol content of almost 75 percent. This distillate is transferred by the cellar or Calvados master to large oaken casks where it undergoes a highly controlled aging process. As with the other brandies, the aging of Calvados is an art. Although some producers age their Calvados for only one year, many choose to age it in oak longer. The distiller who purchases my father's apples ages his Calvados for a minimum of two years but sometimes for as long as fifty-four years.

Calvados is often started in young casks and later transferred to older, aged ones. During this time the clear distillate begins to assume some of the qualities alive in the oak and by degree turns a rich amber hue. It is during this aging process that the Calvados master begins the blending of the young brandy with older, more self-assured Calvados. Because of this requisite blending, the vintage of a bottle of Calvados is not important; if the Calvados master is skilled, there should be little difference from one year to the next. This process—helped along by the addition of a little distilled water—reduces the high alcohol content of the Calvados to a drinkable 40 percent to 45 percent.

And yet, despite this wealth of spirits surrounding us, we rarely ever purchased professionally distilled Calvados. My father, like most of the other farmers in the area, enjoyed distilling his own Calvados in an old copper still he kept in a shed next to the house. He would age the brandy in a small barrel until he deemed it ready for drinking and then transfer it to bottles containing hazelnuts for added flavor and depth of color.

When company came, a bottle would be brought down

from the cupboard, or even at the end of a meal a little Calvados would be poured into a cup to help wash down the last
few drops of coffee. More often, however, we would all finish
the meal with small cups of grog Calvados—a little hot water,
a tablespoon or two or Calvados, a thin slice of apple, and
perhaps sugar to taste. To this day, I can't think of a much
better way to end a good meal.

Index